America's Four-Corner State's Camping Opportunities

Camping, RV'ing, and Hiking in the American Southwest

Updated October 11, 2018
Now
Over ~~600~~, ~~800~~, ~~900~~, 1,300 Entries

Southwestern Campgrounds, RV Parks, and Hiking Trails

By
William (Bill) C. McElroy
Copyright 2016-2019

ISBN: 9781677472604

Preface

This manual provides an insight into *Campgrounds, RV parks, and Hiking trails* of the southwestern U.S.A.

This e-book provides the reader with over 1,300 locations in the American Southwest *Four-Corner States of Arizona, Colorado, New Mexico, and Utah.*

Included are some of the storage and maintenance facilities for Recreational Vehicles. {Some, but not all are marked as such}

The manual provides the user with GPS locations. Hiking trails frequently start from a road or street and then branch out into other trails with other names. Thus, many of the trails ONLY have GPS coordinates as each starts or stops in the wilderness, and NOT at an access road.

This manual is for planning purposes, and one has to understand that road and weather conditions, businesses going in and out of business, seasonal opens and closings, and other unforeseen factors may effect the actual trip and the information provided here, thus you have my disclaimer and you should verify all information, before leaving home.

Note:

The names and locations, including the GPS coordinates are from Google Maps™ and are the results of weeks of research; there may be locations not listed, and locations listed that are not available. No RV camp or service has paid for this listing, and the information is supplied to you, my reader, as of Oct 2018 for 'informational purposes only', the responsibility for verifying the data is up to you.

Kindle Users

This database of Campgrounds, RV Parks, and Hiking Trails provides hundreds of names, street addresses, towns, postal Zip codes, and Global Positioning System (GPS) references. Amazon Kindle e-books have a *'Search'* provision that will allow you to search on any of the data within.

To find a specific location use the name into the *'Search'* box, the program will find the information for you. If you do NOT know the specific name of the location, then type in the postal Zip, or the Town name, or the street address, or GPS number. This will provide you with a listing of the parks and trails at the location you plan on visiting or you seek.

Once you have the name and location GPS, you can enter that number or name into a Mapping program like Google Maps tm along with your starting location and find the best route, the driving times, and the distance to the location(s) you seek from any GPS location in Canada, Mexico, Central America, or the United States.

Table of Contents

Hiking Trails & Vacations

The American Southwest has some of the finest hiking trails in the world, these trails range from a few miles in length to hundreds of miles in length.

The *Arizona National Scenic Trail* is one of the longest and transcends Arizona from its northern border at Utah to its southern border with Mexico, some 800 miles. It crosses the Colorado River in the Grand Canyon, and covers deserts, mountains, forest, grasslands, and valleys.

{Picture - Rhyolite Trail, Chiricahua National Park, Willcox, Arizona}

Other trails are mostly day trails that are within public parks and take from about an hour to a day to hike; these trails can be easy to moderate to rough, and you need to read up on the conditions of each, BEFORE you try the hike.

Caution:

Hiking in the American Southwest can be dangerous, there is not only the roughness of some of the trails, but there are cacti, snakes, dangerous plants and insects, and a lack of facilities and water. Emergency services are great, but only if you have a means of notifying each. Cell phone service may NOT be available in every area, thus always inform people where you are hiking and when you plan to begin the hike and return. Hike in Teams of two or more.

Weather is a prime factor as well, it can easily reach over 110 degrees F.; Monsoon Rains miles away can cause flooding of trails; and many trails are closed in the winter due to heavy snowfalls. Remember that it can be many degrees colder at higher elevations, i.e., Mt Lemmon in Tucson.

In Addition, if near the U.S.A. - Mexican Border wilderness areas, you must be on the lookout for 'illegals' {drug trade mostly, selling to U.S.A. citizens} as these people can be dangerous.

Note that the GPS coordinates are from *Google Maps*®, and each is presumed to be either an entry point, starting point, or ending point of a trail; but some trails are up to hundreds of miles in length, and therefore only portions are listed, i.e., *Arizona {National} Scenic Trail for* example

Check the beginning and ending points, and do a *Mileage Check* of the portion you are to be hiking; a ten-mile hike up a canyon becomes a 20-mile hike if you have to return. Additionally, do you have transportation waiting on the exit side of a one-way hike?

Arizona Campgrounds, RV Parks, and Hiking Trails

Arizona Campgrounds & RV Parks

A Bar A RV Park and Storage
N Tangerine Lane
Marana, AZ 85658
32.425463, -111.157263

A-1 Affordable RV & Mini Storage
{Not a campground, but an RV facility}
3702 Hwy 260
Camp Verde, AZ 86322
34.618387, -111.918222

Access Boat & RV Storage
{Not a campground, but an RV facility}
2200 Rancho Colorado Blvd
Bullhead City, AZ 86442
35.125104, -114.576771

Adobe Village RV Park
11350 S Payson Drive
Yuma, AZ 85365
32.665901, -114.453686

Adventure Bound Camping Resorts
10195 S Houghton Road
Tucson, AZ 85747
32.067888, -110.764423

Affinity RV Services Sales & Rentals

{Not a campground, but an RV facility}
1050 Arizona 69
Dewey, AZ 86327
34.527669, - 112.242141

Ajo Heights RV Park

2000 N Ajo Gila Bend Hwy
Ajo, AZ 85321
32.393333, -112.871267

All Mountain RV Service & Supply

{Not a campground, but an RV facility}
5621 Hwy 260
Lakeside, AZ 85929
34.191236, - 110.014992

All RV Services Center

{Not a campground, but an RV facility}
537 W Grant Road
Tucson, AZ 85705
32.249968, -110.980263

Al's RV Park Rental & Motel

510 Riggles Avenue
Quartzsite, AZ 85346
33.660932, -114.199850

American Trails RV Park

310 N Central Blvd
Quartzsite, AZ 85346
33.671724, -114.217603

Apache Trout Campground

Arizona
33.869040, -109.416802

Arcadia Campground

~ 32.672196,-109.884449

Arizona Acres Mobile Home Park and RV Resort

9421 E Main Street
Mesa, AZ 85207
33.413664, -111.626699

Arizona Hideaway RV Park and Campground

18428 S Picacho Hwy
Picacho, AZ 5141
32.712262, -111.499478

Arizona Oasis RV Resort

50238 Ehrenberg Poston Hwy
Ehrenberg, AZ 85334
33.606004, - 114.525030

Arizona Sands RV

E 32nd Street
Yuma, AZ 85365
32.670950, -114.539223

Arizona Sunset RV Park

67330 U.S. 60
Salome, AZ 85348
33.787297, -113.602912

Arizonian (RV) Resort

15976 U.S. 60
Apache Junction, AZ 85118
33.299967, -111.394208

Arrowhead RV Resort

30115 Wellton Mohawk Drive
Wellton, AZ 85356
32.674174, -114.118478

Aztec Mobile Home & RV Park

401 E Wickenburg Way
Wickenburg, AZ 85390
33.971280, -112.724116

Benson I-10 RV Park

840 N Ocotillo Road
Benson, AZ 85602
31.980744, -110.305444

Benson KOA

180 W 4 Feathers Lane
Benson, AZ 85602
31.988166,-110.302146

Best Auto RV & Truck Repair

{Not a campground, but an RV facility}
585 N Central
Quartzsite, AZ 85346
33.676546, -114.217088

Bishop's Trailer Sales

{Not a campground, but an RV facility}

538 Old W Hwy
Apache Junction, AZ 85119
33.410148, -111.540039

Black Barts RV Park

2760 E Butler Avenue
Flagstaff, AZ 86004
35.193648, -111.616377

Black Canyon City KOA

19600 St Joseph Road
Black Canyon City, AZ 85324
34.040596,-112.139540

Black Rock RV Village

46751 U.S. 60
Salome, AZ 85348
33.679474, -113.945378

Blue Diamond Home & RV

5758 Hwy 260
Lakeside, AZ 85929
34.192917, -110.015843

Blue Diamond Home & RV

5676 E 32nd Street
Yuma, AZ 85365
32.670748, -114.534909

Blue Sky R.V. Park

10247 E Frontage Road
Yuma, AZ 85365
32.669929, -114.456548

Branson's Motel Marina RV

7804 Riverside Drive
Parker, AZ 85344
34.220040, -114.198830

Brenda RV Resort

46251 U.S. 60
Salome, AZ 85348
33.679332, -113.953752

Budget RV Park

2024 S Cortez Road
Apache Junction, AZ 85219
33.396677, -111.520519

Bullhead RV Park

1610 Arizona 95
Bullhead City, AZ 86442
35.127091, -114.574979

Burrwood RV Park, Burwood RV.

Quartzsite, AZ 85346
33.674468, -114.202962

Butterfield RV Resort

251 S Ocotillo Avenue
Benson, AZ 85602
31.968168, -110.307035

Cactus RV Wash & Detail

{Not a campground, but an RV facility}
419 W 9th Street
Casa Grande, AZ 85122

32.881273, -111.758967

Camelot RV Park

651 N Main Street
Cottonwood, AZ 86326
34.744888, -112.017582

CampGround Buena Tierra

1995 S Cox Road
Casa Grande, AZ 85122
32.831984, -111.688748

Campground

Cochise, AZ 85606
Cochise Stronghold
31.925100, -109.967276

Canyon Gateway RV Park

1060 N Grand Canyon Blvd
Williams, AZ 86046
35.264053, - 112.192002

Canyon Lake Marina and Campground

16802 AZ-88,
Apache Junction, AZ 85119
33.534406, -111.422533

Canyon Motel & RV Park

1900 E Rodeo Road
Williams, AZ 86046
35.258909, -112.171501

Canyon Point Campground

Forest Lakes
Estates, AZ 85931
34.324725, -110.826632

Canyon Vista RV Resort

6601 U.S. 60
Gold Canyon, AZ 85118
33.362377, -111.474487

Casa Grande RV Resort

195 W Rodeo Road
Casa Grande, AZ 85222
32.921422, -111.754836

Castle Rock Shores (RV

5220 Arizona 95
Parker, AZ 85344
34.257552, -114.143417

Cave Spring Campground

Sedona, AZ 86336
34.999089, -111.739975

Chavez Crossing Campground

Oak Creek Cliffs Drive, Sedona, AZ 86336
34.843219, -111.777218

Clear Creek Campground

Forest Road 626
Camp Verde, AZ 86322
34.515792, -111.768728

Clint's Well Campground,

National Forest Road Route 3
Flagstaff, AZ 86024
34.554996, -111.315648

Coach Stop RV Park

30333 Wellton Mohawk Drive
Wellton, AZ 85356
32.675385, -114.118886

Cochise Terrace RV Resort

1030 Barrel Cactus Ridge
Benson, AZ 85602
31.949628, -110.344956

Copper Mountain RV Park

Tacna, AZ 85352
32.687867, -113.954429

Cottonwood Cove Mobile Home & RV Park

426 W Cottonwood Lane
Casa Grande, AZ 85222
32.895048, -111.760070

Country RV

5486 Wild Game Trail
Lakeside, AZ 85929
34.192598, -110.015220

Cousin Terry's RV & Auto

{Not a campground, but an RV facility}
4532 Arizona 95
Fort Mohave, AZ 86426

35.025028, -114.597809

Covered Wagon RV Park

6540 N Black Canyon Hwy
Phoenix, AZ 85017
33.532252, - 112.113147

Crazy Horse Campground

Lake Havasu City, AZ 86403
34.469076, -114.357592

Crazy Horse RV Park

6660 S Craycroft Road
Tucson, AZ 85756
32.131352, -110.876282

Crook Campground

5925 Wagon Wheel Lane
Pinetop-Lakeside, AZ 85929
34.317618, -110.942544

De Anza RV Resort

2869 Interstate 19 Frontage Road
Amado, AZ 85645
31.705492, - 111.062775

Deer Valley Mini & RV Storage

{Not a campground, but an RV facility}
1930 W Adobe Drive
Phoenix, AZ 85027
33.687534, - 112.101161

Desert Cypress Mobile Home and RV Park

610 Jack Burden Road
Wickenburg, AZ 85390
33.974154, -112.725500

Desert Gem RV Park

64508 U.S. 60
Salome, AZ 85348
33.759324, -113.653670

Desert Gold RV Resort

46628 U.S. 60
Salome, AZ 85348
33.677689, -113.946751

Desert Pueblo Mobile Home & RV Park

1302 W Ajo Way
Tucson, AZ 85713
32.178115, -110.992257

Desert Sands RV Park

22036 N 27th Avenue
Phoenix, AZ 85027
33.687007, -112.118547

Desert Trails RV Park

3200-3398 Sunset View Trail
Tucson, AZ 85735
32.181258, -111.149269

Desert Valley RV Resort

4555 W Tonto Road
Eloy, AZ 85131

Desert View Campground

Grand Canyon Village, AZ 86023
36.038877,-111.822624
32.785499, -111.629274

Desert's Edge RV Village

2398 W Williams Drive
Phoenix, AZ 85027
33.691698, -112.110641

Devil's Canyon Campground

{Alkali Point / Manti-La Sal National Forest, Monticello, UT 84535}
37.729181,-109.412091 / 37.738956,-109.406279

Diamond Creek Campground

Peach Springs, AZ 86434
35.765829, -113.370843
This in on the Native American reservation and is the launching point for
Colorado / Grand Canyon Rafting offered by the Hualapai tribe.

Diamond Creek Junction Campground

Whiteriver, AZ 85941
33.893689, -109.934264

Diamond Creek Number Two Campground

Whiteriver, AZ 85941
33.907913, -109.919017

Dillons RV Sales & Storage

300 N Ocotillo Road
Benson, AZ 85602

31.971856, -110.306563

Distant Drums RV Resort

581 W Middle Verde Road
Camp Verde, AZ 86322
34.613867, -111.863823

Dogtown Lake Campground

1250 S Pine Top Drive
Williams, AZ 86046
35.208794, -112.127793

Encinoso Picnic Area

AZ 89A - GPS 34.924764,-111.735383

Fairgrounds RV Park

10443 Arizona 89A
Prescott Valley, AZ 86315
34.647796, -112.283107

Flagstaff Area National Monument Park Headquarters

6400 N Hwy 89
Flagstaff, AZ 86004
35.238980, -111.570806

Flagstaff KOA

5803 U.S. 89
Flagstaff, AZ 86004
35.233903, -111.577133

Foothill Village RV Resort

12705 S Frontage Road
Yuma, AZ 85365
32.669228, -114.413030

Fort Beale RV Park

300 Metcalfe Road
Kingman, AZ 86401
35.192179, -114.065390

Fort Tuthill Campground

2446 Fort Tuthill
(Flagstaff Urban - University Heights to Fort Tuthill)
Flagstaff, AZ 86005
35.144383, -111.690740

Fort Willcox RV Park

1765 W Fort Willcox Loop
Willcox, AZ 85643
32.229788, -109.859121

Freedom RV

7475 N I-10 Expressway
Tucson, AZ 85712
32.342198, -111.072622

Gabaldon Horse Camp

Greer, AZ 85927
33.929010, -109.486618

Galpin Ford & RV

920 Arizona 69
Dewey, AZ 86327

34.529632, -112.242892

Gila County RV Park

201 W Cottonwood Street
Globe, AZ 85501
33.393990, -110.787616

Gold Canyon RV & Golf Resort

7151 U.S. 60
Gold Canyon, AZ 85118
33.356597, - 111.468845

Golden Valley RV Park

3532 W Agua Fria Drive
Golden Valley, AZ 86413
35.242201, - 114.148357

Good Sam RV

700 N Central Blvd
Quartzsite, AZ 85346
33.660468, -114.217047

Grand Canyon Camper Village

549 Camper Village Lane
Grand Canyon Village, AZ 86023
35.975207, -112.123913

Grand Canyon Railway RV Park

601 W Franklin Ave.
Williams, AZ 86046
35.250292, - 112.196626

Green Acres RV Park

28400 E County 10th Street
Wellton, AZ 85356
32.678036, -114.153585

Hasslers RV

RV Park Road
Quartzsite, AZ 85346
33.667694, -114.224504

Havasu Springs Campground

2581 Arizona 95
Parker, AZ 85344
34.295981, -114.127065

Havasupai Campground Rangers Office

Arizona 86435
36.256118, -112.700362

Holbrook - Petrified Forest KOA

102 Hermosa Drive
Holbrook, AZ 86025
34.923309, -110.143599

Holiday Palms RV Park

355 W Main Street
Quartzsite, AZ 85346
33.665571, -114.222972

Hometown RV

5610 E 32nd Street

Yuma, AZ 85365
32.670459, -114.535617

Hospitality RV Park & Boarding Stable

51802 U.S. Highways 60/89
Wickenburg, AZ 85390
33.953412, -112.709252

Houston Mesa Campground

Payson, AZ 85541
34.270471, -111.315889

Islander RV Resort

751 Beachcomber Blvd
Lake Havasu City, AZ 86403
34.454246, - 114.361201

J and H RV Park

7901 U.S. 89
Flagstaff, AZ 86004
35.253201, -111.555698

Jones Water Campground

Tonto National Forest, Globe, AZ 85501
{Warning "No Turnaround, Vehicles over 20 Ft. Not Recommended"}
33.588814,-110.647272

Juan Santa Cruz Picnic Area

{Brown Mountain Trail}
N Kinney Rd, Tucson, AZ 85743
32.239417, -111.165919

Kit Carson RV Park

2101 W Rte 66
Flagstaff, AZ 86001
35.187618, -111.679699

Knoll Lake Campground

Payson, AZ 85541
34.427499, -111.092705

Krazy K RV Park

2075 N Arena Del Loma
Camp Verde, AZ 86322
34.599655, -111.871279

La Hacienda RV Resort

1797 W 28th Avenue
Apache Junction, AZ 85120
33.388672, -111.565524

La Mirage RV Park

110 N Washington Avenue
Quartzsite, AZ 85346
33.668990, -114.219140

La Siesta Campgrounds

16005 W Hardscrabble Road
Arivaca, AZ 85601
31.583366, -111.306883

La Siesta Motel & RV Resort

2561 N Ajo Gila Bend Hwy
Ajo, AZ 85321

32.403189, -112.872909

Lake Havasu RV Park

3829 London Bridge Road
Lake Havasu City, AZ 86404
34.544641, - 114.365486

Lake Powell View RV & Boat Storage

70 N Wahweap Drive
Page, AZ 86040
36.995282, -111.565303

Las Colinas Motor Home-RV Resort

7136 S Sunland Gin Road
Eloy, AZ 85131
32.814795, -111.674172

Lazy Coyote RV Village

28541 Arizona Avenue
Wellton, AZ 85356
32.671092, -114.148943

Lower Wolf Creek Campground

344 S Cortez Street
Prescott, AZ 86303
34.456718, -112.490825

Magic Circle RV Park

700 Virginia Ave
Willcox, AZ 85643
32.264200, -109.847165

Many Trails RV

6850 Arizona 69
Prescott Valley, AZ 86314
34.583522, -112.345194

Mather Campground

1 Village Loop Road
Canyon Village, AZ 86023
36.049995, -112.120488

Mesa - Apache Junction KOA

1540 S Tomahawk Road
Apache Junction, AZ 85119
33.401579,-111.530297

Meteor Crater RV Park

I 40 Meteor Crater Road
Winslow, AZ 86047
35.106760 - 111.032658

Midvale Park RV & Self Storage

6565 S Headley Road Tucson
AZ 85746
32.132215, -111.007316

Morenga Palms RV Park

Morenga Palms
Wenden, AZ 85357
33.822509, -113.541603

Mountain View RV Park

1120 E Business Loop
Bowie, AZ 85605

32.329741, -109.502626

Mountain View RV Park

99 W Vista Lane
Huachuca City, AZ 85616
31.683468, -110.353035

Mountain View RV Ranch

2843 Interstate 19 Frontage Road
Amado, AZ 85645
31.703410, - 111.063937

Noon Creek Campground

~ 32.667877,-109.797205

Normas RV Park

4572 Main Street
Joseph City, AZ 86032
34.956110, -110.327534

North Phoenix Campground

2550 W Louise Drive
Phoenix, AZ 85027
33.686043, -112.114416

Oak Flat Campground

Superior, AZ 85173
33.308122, -111.050183

Oak Park Motel and RV Park

22658 Arizona 89
Yarnell, AZ 85362

34.220903, -112.748168

Orangewood RV Center
11449 W Bell Road
Surprise, AZ 85378
33.637970, -112.305612

Page-Lake Powell Campground
849 S Coppermine Road
Page, AZ 86040
36.901757, -111.453146

Palm Drive Mobile Home & RV
550 Palm Drive
Wickenburg, AZ 85390
33.976173, -112.740965

Park Place RV Park
205 N Riggles Avenue
Quartzsite, AZ 85346
33.672040, -114.200215

Park'n Shade RV & Boat Storage
{Not a campground, but an RV facility}
7935 W Tangerine Road
Marana, AZ 85658
32.422402, -111.134413

Pato Blanco Lakes RV Park & Resort
635 E Pearl Street
Benson, AZ 85602
31.970899, - 110.288116

Paul's Southeast Arizona RV Rentals

LLC, 460 Arizona 82
Huachuca City, AZ 85616
31.692442, -110.338766

Payson Campground & RV Resort

808 Arizona 260
Payson, AZ 85541
34.243544, -111.310467

Phoenix RV Consignment Specialists

12495 NW Grand Avenue
El Mirage, AZ 85335
33.620877, -112.328687

Pine Creek RV Park & Mini Storage

3584 Arizona 87
Pine, AZ 85544
34.382785, -111.453178

Pine Flat Campground

12240 Arizona 89A
Sedona, AZ 86336
35.011972, -111.738565

Pine Lawn Ranch Mobile Home & RV Park

910 W Gurley Street
Prescott, AZ 86305
34.543352, -112.483411

Pioneer RV Resort

36408 N Black Canyon Hwy
Phoenix, AZ 85086

33.822614, -112.148351

Pirates Den RV Resort and Marina

7350 Riverside Drive
Parker, AZ 85344
34.224422, - 114.191963

Pleasant Harbor RV - Go Sail Arizona

8708 W Harbor Blvd
Peoria, AZ 85383
33.846187, -112.252034

Potato Patch Campground

Jerome, AZ 86331
34.709521, -112.155299

Premier RV & Self Storage

22230 N Black Canyon Hwy
Phoenix, AZ 85027
33.688078, - 112.113625

Prince of Tucson RV Park

3501 North Freeway
Tucson, AZ 85705
32.270217, -111.011337

Prospectors RV Resort & Spa

4750 London Bridge Road
Lake Havasu City, AZ 86404
34.560034, -114.369842

Quail Ridge RV Resort

2207 N Yucca Drive
Huachuca City, AZ 85616
31.688790, -110.355482

Quarter Horse RV & Motel

800 W 4th Street
Benson, AZ 85602
31.971278, -110.312174

Queen Mine RV Park

473 N Dart Road
Bisbee, AZ 85603
31.439936, -109.912479

Railside RV Ranch

877 E Rodeo Road
Williams, AZ 86046
35.258490, -112.180060

Ramblin' Roads RV Resorts

60655 U.S. 60
Salome, AZ 85348
33.722827, -113.704104

Rancho Sedona RV Park

135 Bear Wallow Lane,
Sedona, AZ 86336
34.866458, -111.760044

Rancho Verde RV Park

1488 W Horseshoe Bend Drive
Camp Verde, AZ 86322

34.600855, -111.883731

Red Barn Campground
711 Madison Street
Benson, AZ 85602
31.979079, -110.301034

Rincon Country East RV Resort
8989 E Escalante Road
Tucson, AZ 85730
32.177647, -110.801465

Rio Verde RV Park
3420 Arizona 89A
Cottonwood, AZ 86326
34.721797, -111.989882

Rio Vista Boat & RV Storage
31647 Storage Place
Parker, AZ 85344
34.185899, -114.221424

River Breeze RV Resort
50202 Ehrenberg Parker Hwy
Ehrenberg, AZ 85334
33.606844, - 114.522863

River Lagoon (RV) Resort
50078 Ehrenberg Poston Hwy
Ehrenberg, AZ 85334
33.609695, - 114.520491

Rose Canyon Campground

Catalina Hwy,
Tucson, AZ 85619
32.393108, -110.704546

Rose Garden Mobile Home Resort

11596 Sierra Dawn Blvd
Surprise, AZ 85374
33.636308, - 112.309453

Rose RV Park

600 Kuehn Street
Quartzsite, AZ 85342
33.660664, -114.207082

Ruthrauff RV

2750 W Ruthrauff Road
Tucson, AZ 85705
32.294845, -111.025836

RV City Inc

2095 Arizona 90
Huachuca City, AZ 85616
31.683550, -110.351576

RV Pitstop

425 N Central Blvd
Quartzsite, AZ 85346
33.673581, -114.216766

RV Traders

11111 E Apache Trail
Apache Junction, AZ 85120

33.414365, -111.590879

RV World Recreation Vehicle
5875 E Gila Ridge Road
Yuma, AZ 85365
32.675409, - 114.531347

Saddle Mountain RV Park Inc
40902 W Osborn Road
Tonopah, AZ 85354
33.487558, -112.932654

Safari Mobile Home RV Park
120 E O'Neil Drive
Casa Grande, AZ 85122
32.898867, - 111.754319

Salome KOA - Desert Vista RV Resort
64812 Harcuvar Drive
Salome, AZ 85348
33.760903, -113.649089

Sandy's Restaurant & RV Park
5120 Arizona 181
Pearce, AZ 85625
31.884085, -109.694079

Sandy's West RV Center
1451 W Miracle Mile
Tucson, AZ 85705
32.260885, -110.997275

Seligman Route 66 KOA

21305 Interstate 40 Business Loop
Seligman, AZ 86337
35.322462, -112.854114

Sharp Creek Camp Grounds

Payson, AZ 85541
34.303500, -110.999847

Sheep Crossing Campground

Greer, AZ 85927
33.959787, -109.506476

Show Low Lake Campground

5800 Show Low Lake Rd
Lakeside, AZ 85929
34.195570, -110.007366

Sinkhole Campground, Hwy 260

Payson, AZ 85541
34.305337, -110.886787

Snow Flat Boy Scout Camp

~ 32.652939,-109.86466

South Cove RV Resort

410 Diamond Creek Drive
Meadview, AZ 86444
36.009205, -114.072472

South Forty RV Ranch

3614-3620 W Orange Grove Road

Tucson, AZ 85741
32.323285, -111.041711

Southwest RV - Service Parts Storage Inc.

17030 N 63rd Avenue
Glendale, AZ 85308
33.640090, -112.196005

Spillway Campground

Woods Canyon
Road Forest Lakes
Estates, AZ 85931
34.332540, -110.940416

Stampede RV Park

201 W Allen Street
Tombstone, AZ 85638
31.714155, -110.072076

Strawberry RV & Trailer Park

Strawberry, AZ 85544
34.407411, -111.494250

Sun City RV

9045 NW Grand Avenue
Sun City, AZ 85345
33.591469, -112.253668

Sun City RV Compound

16315 N 115th Avenue
Surprise, AZ 85378

Sun Country RV Park

10321 Fresno Street
Wellton, AZ 85356
32.672915, -114.137701

Sun Ridge RV Park

10347 E 34th Street
Yuma, AZ 85365
32.665314, -114.455800

Sun Valley RV Park

Sun Valley, AZ 86025
34.981393, -110.056151

Sunrise RV Park

3131 Mac Donald Avenue
Kingman, AZ
35.216322, -114.013688

Sunset Palms RV Park

11450 S Payson Drive
Yuma, AZ 85365
32.664076, -114.453740

Superior RV Park

1113 U.S. 60
Superior, AZ 85173
Permanently closed?

Ten X Campground

Grand Canyon Village, AZ 86023
35.937978,-112.122647

Tews & Date Palm RV Park

1360 N Moon Mountain Avenue
Quartzsite, AZ 85346
33.685955, -114.225667

The RV Store

1530 N Pinal Avenue
Casa Grande, AZ 85122
32.891776, -111.756830

The Scenic Road RV Park

480 N Central Blvd
Quartzsite, AZ 85346
33.674564, -114.217453

Tier Drop RV Park

28320 E County 11th Street
Wellton, AZ 85356
32.665153, -114.154825

Timber Camp

Globe, AZ 85501
33.688412, -110.571706

Tombstone RV Campground

Tombstone, AZ 85638
31.730687, -110.079472

Trails End RV Park

983 Finnie Flat Road
Camp Verde, AZ 86322
34.565374, -111.870671

Trailer Village

100 Market Plaza Road
Grand Canyon Village, AZ 86023
36.052424, -112.113683

Tucson Truck & RV Wash

{Not a campground, but an RV facility}
5445 E Benson Hwy
Tucson, AZ 85706
32.134795, -110.892190

Turquoise Hills Golf & RV

800 Country Club Road
Benson, AZ 85602
31.950002, - 110.280771

Turquoise Triangle RV Park

Cottonwood, AZ 86326-5302
34.720897, -111.999098

Twin Buttes Mobile Home and RV Community

4027 N Twin Buttes Ct.,
Douglas, AZ 85607
31.380493, -109.742903

Tyson Wells RV Park

121 Kuehn Street
Quartzsite, AZ 85346
33.660857, -114.218956

USFS Playground Group Campground

Forest 104 Route
Sedona, AZ 86336

34.697611, -112.136714

Valley of the Sun Mobile Home & RV Park

13377 N Sandario Road
Marana, AZ 85653
32.450935, -111.218857

Valley Vista RV Resort

1060 Arizona 80
Benson, AZ 85602
31.950557, -110.286013

Vans RV Trailer Company

11565 W Bell Road
Surprise, AZ 85378
33.637968, -112.309228

Verde Valley RV & Camping Resort

6400 E Thousand Trails Rd, Cottonwood, AZ 86326
34.671736, -111.940888

Wagon West RV Park

50126 U.S. 60
Salome, AZ 85348
33.778748, -113.618156

Wahweap RV Park

100 Lake Shore Drive
Page, AZ 86040
36.997926, -111.496576

Weavers Needle Travel Trailer

250 S Tomahawk Road
Apache Junction, AZ 85119
33.413355, -111.530861

Western Sands RV Park

10460 E 34th Street
Yuma, AZ 85365
32.668114, -114.453962

Westwind RV & Golf Resort

9797 E 32nd Street
Yuma, AZ 85365
32.668557, -114.463071

Whispering Palms RV Park

3445 N Romero Road
Tucson, AZ 85705
32.270305, -111.003719

Wickiup Mobile Home & RV Park

E Old W Hwy
Apache Junction, AZ 85219
33.398505, - 111.523952

Williams Circle Pines KOA

1000 Circle Pines Road
Williams, AZ 86046
35.259960, -112.116382

Willow Lake RV Park

1617 Heritage Park Road
Prescott, AZ 86301

34.612123, -112.437086

Winn Campground
State Road 273, Greer, AZ 85927
33.964459, -109.486698

Woody Mountain Campground & RV Park
2727 Historic Route 66
Flagstaff, AZ 86001
35.188582, -111.689698

Yuma Mesa RV Park
5990 E 32nd Street
Yuma, AZ 85365
32.670929, -114.531390

Zane Grey RV Park
4500 Hwy 260
Camp Verde, AZ 86322
34.516878, -111.774822

Arizona Hiking Trails

Agate House Trail

Holbrook, AZ 86025
34.808914, -109.859297

Agua Caliente Trail

Arizona 85749
32.275120, -110.712263

Allen's Bend Trail

Sedona, AZ 86336
34.888192, -111.731522

Alta Trail

Laveen Village, AZ 85339
33.330337, -112.144175

Anasazi Spur

Scottsdale, AZ 85259
33.602327, -111.809551

Apache Wash Trailhead

 E Sonoran Desert Drive,
Phoenix, AZ 85085
33.767362, -112.045259

Arizona Hot Springs {Trail}

Willow Beach, AZ 86445
35.975704, -114.704774

Arizona National Scenic Trail

This is a hiking trail that runs north and south the length of Arizona, and it starts at the U.S.A. / Mexican Border, and ends at the Utah state line. GPS 31.996725, -110.652767

Arizona Scenic Trail

Patagonia, AZ 85624
31.527981, -110.711287

Arizona Scenic Trail

Flagstaff, AZ 86001
35.211014, -111.639943

Arrowhead Point

Glendale, AZ 85308
33.691850, -112.184405

Avery-Bryce Trail

Tucson, AZ 85735
32.213688, -111.130532

Bajada Wash Trail

Tucson, AZ 85745
32.271349, -111.209767

Bear Canyon Trail

Tucson, AZ 85749
32.312803, -110.797973

Bell Pass Trail

Scottsdale, AZ 85255
33.646930, -111.836855

Bell Rock Trail

Sedona, AZ 86336
34.792407, -111.762135

Bixler Trail

Ash Fork, AZ 86320
35.215958, -112.481615

Black Canyon Trail

Mayer, AZ 86333
34.342061, -112.187300

Black Canyon Trail
Spring Valley, AZ 86333
34.370136, -112.172403

Blodgett Basin Trailhead

Camp Verde-Payson Highway
Camp Verde, AZ 86322
34.538694, -111.689773

Bluff Trail

Scottsdale, AZ 85262
33.696788, -111.776255

Boulder Canyon Trailhead

Apache Trail, Apache Junction, AZ 85119
33.534083, -111.422804

Boulder Trail

Fountain Hills, AZ 85268
33.684388, -111.787489

Bowen Trail

Tucson, AZ 85745
32.215309, -111.052493

Box Canyon Loop

Phoenix, AZ 85042
33.350543, -112.073669

Boyce Thompson Arboretum State Park

37615 U.S. 60,
Superior, AZ 85273
33.279402, -111.158785

Brown Mountain Trail Picnic Area and Trailhead

Brown Mountain Trail,
Tucson, AZ 85743
32.229696, -111.145180

Bud Gode Interpretive Nature Trail

Green Valley, AZ 85614
31.733751, -110.882400

Buena Vista Trailhead - Moderate-Loop

Mogollon Rim Road,
Show Low, AZ 85901
34.204343, -110.080409

Buffalo Park Loop

Flagstaff, AZ 86004
35.220269, -111.632348

Buffalo Park Loop

Flagstaff, AZ 86004
35.222972, -111.631798

Bug Spring Trailhead

Catalina Hwy, AZ 85619
32.345084, -110.718234

Bursera {trail}

Phoenix, AZ 85045
33.306630, -112.098425

Caballo Trail

Scottsdale, AZ 85255
33.694544, -111.794755

Cactus Canyon Trail

Tucson, AZ 85745
32.312803, -111.127025

Cactus Wren Trail

Tucson, AZ 85743
32.290967, -111.208195

Call of the Canyon Trail

Sedona, AZ 86336
34.990713, -111.742968

Calloway Trail

{Hunter Trail}
Picacho, AZ 85141
32.642706, -111.402566

Cam-Boh Trail

Tucson, AZ 85743
32.319373, -111.165953

Camino de Oeste Trailhead

N Camino De Oeste, Tucson, AZ 85745
32.226579, -111.062841

Carrie Nation Mine Trail

Green Valley, AZ 85614
31.712540, -110.873797

Casner Canyon Trail

Sedona, AZ 86336
34.893153, -111.732807

Cat Mountain Trail

Tucson, AZ 85713
32.182208, -111.047017

Catalina State Park, (CSP) Tucson, Arizona

CSP-Bird Trail (This is a bird watching area)
32.424632,-110.9074

CSP-Canyon Loop Trail (Most popular trail, ~ 1.4 mile loop)
32.425632,-110.907838

CSP-Foot trail (Ruins along path?)
32.419783,-110.928205

CSP-Romano Canyon Trail (Water pools and waterfalls in season)
32.422606,-110.8953

CSP-Melrose Canyon Trail
32.422606,-110.8953

CSP-Sutherland Trail parking area
32.452938, -110.890822

Cathedral Rock Trailhead

Back O Beyond Road, Sedona, AZ 86336
34.825236, -111.788423

Cheops Trail

Tucson, AZ 85745
32.220168, -111.107343

Children's Cave Trail

Picacho, AZ 85141
32.645170, -111.405532

Chuparosa Trail

Scottsdale, AZ 85262
33.711981, -111.720575

Cienega Bridge

Vail, Arizona - Gabe Zimmerman Trail
Cienega Bridge,

Vail, Arizona - Arizona National Scenic Trail
32.014117, -110.647617

Coachwhip, {trail}

Glendale, AZ 85308
33.674324, -112.169578

Cosmo Dog Park

2502 E Ray Road,
Gilbert, AZ 85296
33.322629, -111.734959

Coyote Pass Trail

Tucson, AZ 85745
32.314660, -111.129144

David Yetman West Trailhead,

Tucson, AZ 85735
32.217308, -111.102875

Dead Man's Pass {trail},

Laveen Village, AZ 85339
33.334021, -112.146197

Desert Classic Trail,

Phoenix, AZ 85042
33.322917, -112.066618

Desert Classic Trail,

Phoenix, AZ 85042
33.316145, -112.057135

Dirt Path,

Show Low, AZ 85901
34.202729, -110.007088

Dixie Mine Trail,

Fountain Hills, AZ 85268
33.653364, -111.787327

East End Trail,

Scottsdale, AZ 85255
33.689244, -111.805326

Echo Canyon Trail

{Chiricahua National Monument}
Willcox, AZ 85643
32.011808, -109.315780

Eliminator II Trail

Phoenix, AZ 85042
33.321132, -112.100586

Encinas Trail

Tucson, AZ 85743
32.306193, -111.216456

Explorer Trail

Tucson, AZ 85713
32.178194, -111.044446

Flagstaff Loop Trail

Flagstaff, AZ 86001
35.150313, -111.697041

Fort Tuthill-Palmer Bypass

Flagstaff, AZ 86001
35.164312, -111.674591

Fossil Springs Trail Head

Fossil Creek Road,
Pine, AZ 85544
34.406739, -111.568312

FUTS {Trail to Arizona Trail}

Flagstaff, AZ 86004
35.167473, -111.632144

Gabe Zimmerman Davidson Canyon Trailhead

This is a trail that is just east of Tucson and north of I-10. It is at the Ciénega Creek Bridge and is a popular pictorial spot for many. GPS 32.014117, -110.647617

Gateway Loop Trail

Scottsdale, AZ 85255
33.649304, -111.852081

Geronimo Trail

Payson, AZ 85541
34.414828, -111.374299

Gila Trail

Phoenix, AZ 85045
33.309201, -112.135602

Goldmine Trail

Queen Creek, AZ 85142
33.167104, -111.637779

Government Tank Road {Trail}

Flagstaff, AZ 86004

Grand Canyon Hiking Trail Itineraries

For those getting out of their vehicles and doing a little walking, this section provides a look at most of the hiking trails that go into or transverse the Grand Canyon from the southern rim to the northern rim.

Bright Angel trail is 10.3 miles to the Bright Angel Campground area. The trail starts at the Grand Canyon Village and winds down the canyon to eventually meet with the Tonto, South and North Kaibab trails and the Phantom Ranch

The 14.2-mile North Kaibab trail runs from the Bright Angel Point Lodge on the North Rim of the canyon to the Phantom Ranch at the Colorado River.

The *Hermit trail* starts at *Hermits Rest* west of *Pima Point* and proceeds 8.9 miles down to the Colorado River.

The *South Kaibab trail* meets the Tonto where one can go west to the *Bright Angel trail* and the *Bright Angel Campground*; about 6.4 miles total.

The *Grandview Trail* starts at *Grandview Point* and drops to the valley floor where it meets the *Tonto Trail.*

The *Tonto Trail* runs parallel to the *Colorado River* for most of its length through the Grand Canyon, but is not maintained and is not for the beginning hiker.

The *Rim Trail* follows the road from the Grand Canyon Village to Hermits Rest.

The *Hance Trail* is a short not maintained trail just west of *Moran Point.*

Beginners should stick to the *Bright Angel* or the *South Kaibab trails* as these are reasonably maintained and frequently traveled. Take plenty of water with you, it gets very hot during the summer months; and do not go swimming in the Colorado as it is swift and deceiving and many hikers and campers have drowned in its waters. Note that it can get very cold, and possibly snow, in the fall, winter, and spring months.

If you are going to make the trip to the *Phantom Ranch*, you will need reservations and you must plan to spend the night. Even the short trips down into the canyon will be a challenge on the climb back out, and you should figure that it will take you twice as long as it did going down to come back up.

When camping hang all foodstuffs high in trees unless you plan on feeding the ground squirrels and other crawling animals that may find your provisions a tasty treat.

You will need a permit from the Park Rangers if you are to go backpacking or doing an overnight, and you should get a copy of the *Backcountry Trip Planner* or join a group like the *Grand Canyon Field Institute*, which offers guided trips into the canyon. There are mule rides and river trips also available.

Grand Enchantment Trail
Willcox, AZ 85643
32.717495, -109.977096

Grand Enchantment Trail
Pima, AZ 85543
32.741631, -110.023993

Granite Trail
Scottsdale, AZ 85262
33.683489, -111.725069

Guano Point Trail
Arizona 86434
36.032764, -113.825053

H-1a Trail

Glendale, AZ 85308
33.695512, -112.178718

Hawk Nest Trail

Scottsdale, AZ 85255
33.726808, -111.795812

Hedgehog Trail

Queen Creek, AZ 85142
33.155483, -111.638696

Helipad to Goat

Phoenix, AZ 85048
33.323068, -112.037805

Hidden Canyon Trail

Tucson, AZ 85745
32.216943, -111.050015

Hieroglyphic Trail

Gold Canyon, AZ 85118
33.389697, -111.424437

Highland Trail

Flagstaff, AZ 86001
35.144926, -111.700255

Highline Trail

Pine, AZ 85544
34.374276, -111.443309

Hilltop Trail

Fort McDowell, AZ 85264
33.689843, -111.717794

Historic Sabino Trail

Tucson, AZ 85718
32.339827, -110.780186

Holbert Trail

Phoenix, AZ 85042
33.351621, -112.069994

Homolovi State Park walking trail

Winslow, AZ 86047
35.045991, -110.652928

Honeymoon Cove Trail

Peoria, AZ 85383
33.859471, -112.251925

Hoot Loop Trailhead

Arizona
34.784405, -111.732437

Hugh Norris Trail

Tucson, AZ 85745
32.271547, -111.203090

Hwy 89A Trailhead

Loy Butte Road,
Arizona 86336
34.817163, -111.904737

Iris O. Dewhirst Pima Canyon Trailhead

Pima Canyon, AZ 85718
32.353355, -110.948251

Iron King Trail

(Prescott to Prescott Valley),
Arizona
34.606534, -112.404391

Jan Alfano Trail

Prescott, AZ 86301
34.593942, -112.432364

Kiwanis Trail

Phoenix, AZ 85042
33.340743, -112.076122

La Milagrosa Canyon Trail

Tucson
32.298160, -110.720846

Lake Mead National Recreation Area

Temple Bar Marina, AZ 86443
36.102896, -114.901281

Las Lomitas {trail}

Phoenix, AZ 85042
33.341011, -112.076391

Lava Flow Trail

Flagstaff, AZ 86004
35.363222, -111.518151

Legends of Superior Trail

Superior, AZ 85173
33.281133, -111.160472

Liberty Bell Arch {Trail}

Willow Beach, AZ 86445
35.975912, -114.704855

Lightning Ridge Trailhead

Greer, AZ 85927
33.920368, -109.448063

Littleleaf Trail

Queen Creek, AZ 85142
33.167570, -111.636237

Long Logs Trail

Holbrook, AZ 86025
34.810381, -109.858288

Lookout Trail

Scottsdale, AZ 85255
33.679538, -111.808840

Lost Dog Wash Parking Lot

N 124th Street,
Scottsdale, AZ 85259
33.599026, -111.813449

Lost Goldmine East Trailhead

10987-10999 E Peralta Road,
Gold Canyon, AZ 85118
33.392315, -111.353978

Lost Ranch Ruins Trail

Phoenix, AZ 85045
33.318442, -112.112828

Lower Corona {trail}

Phoenix, AZ 85042
33.328194, -112.028940

Malpais Trail

Queen Creek, AZ 85142
33.148641, -111.652188

Manuel de Miguell Access Trail

Flagstaff, AZ 86001
35.166621, -111.681802

Manville Trail

Tucson, AZ 85743
32.306112, -111.216563

Marcus Landslide Trail

Scottsdale, AZ 85255
33.684382, -111.787525

Maricopa Trail

Laveen Village, AZ 85339
33.323787, -112.146406

Maricopa Trail

Surprise, AZ 85387
33.685697, -112.412742

Mesquite Canyon Trail

Scottsdale, AZ 85255
33.694385, -111.800457

Moonlight Trail

Queen Creek, AZ 85142
33.161425, -111.652376

Munds Wagon Trail

Sedona, AZ 86336
34.866358, -111.748635

Mystic Trail

Sedona, AZ 86336
34.843780, -111.768052

National Trail

Laveen Village, AZ 85339
33.334030, -112.147852

Nature Center Trail

Peoria, AZ 85383
33.847561, -112.277042

Nature Trail

Picacho, AZ 85141
32.645298, -111.400480

Old Jeep Trail

Scottsdale, AZ 85259
33.610647, -111.807976

Old Man Trail

Phoenix, AZ 85042
33.336862, -112.021786

Old US 93 {Trail}

Willow Beach, AZ 86445
35.980115, -114.697249

Palmer Trail

(Fort Tuthill trail alternative)
Flagstaff, AZ 86001
35.163723, -111.677341

Peavine Trail

(Prescott Peavine Trail)
Prescott, AZ 86301
34.638545, -112.403848

Pemberton Trail

Scottsdale, AZ 85262
33.696775, -111.776274

Pemberton Trail

McDowell, AZ 85262

33.708669, -111.718222

Peralta Trailhead

Peralta Rd, Gold Canyon, AZ 85118
33.397359, -111.347909

Phoneline Trail

Tucson, AZ 85750
32.311398, -110.810116

Picture Rocks Trailhead

{Ringtail Trail}
7768 W Picture Rocks Road
Tucson, AZ 85745
32.327608, -111.130430

Pima Canyon Trail

Tucson, AZ 85718
32.353370, -110.947767

Pipeline Canyon Trail

Morristown, AZ 85342
33.878705, -112.303651

Point of Rocks Campground {Trails}

3025 N State Route 89
Prescott, AZ 86301
34.595438, -112.425874

Potato Patch Loop Trail

Arizona 86401
35.086006, -113.897971

Powerline Road {trail}

Flagstaff, AZ 86001
35.122266, -111.685230

Prescott Legacy Trail

Prescott, AZ 86305
34.615160, -112.466657

Pyramid Trail

Phoenix, AZ 85042
33.305425, -112.100191

Quartz Trail

Scottsdale, AZ 85255
33.620414, -111.864546

Rainbow Forest Museum Trail

Holbrook, AZ 86025
34.815309, -109.865518

Red Mountain Trail

Flagstaff, AZ 86001
35.537019, -111.857928

Richard Genser Starr Pass

Trailhead,
S Avenue Del Correcaminos
Tucson, AZ 85713
32.205370, -111.046654

Richard Genser Starr Pass Trail
Tucson, AZ 85745

32.199215, -111.044351

Ringtail Trail

Scottsdale, AZ 85255
33.605350, -111.813807

Roadrunner Trail

Peoria, AZ 85383
33.847445, -112.277098

Rock Knob Trail

Scottsdale, AZ 85255
33.694514, -111.794153

Rock Peak Wash Trail

Queen Creek, AZ 85142
33.129764, -111.636621

Rock Wren Trail

Tucson, AZ 85735
32.202778, -111.058102

Sabino Canyon Trail

Mt Lemmon, AZ 85619
32.343765, -110.780519

Sabino N Trail

Tucson, AZ 85750
32.316015, -110.816803

Saguaro Loop Trail

Scottsdale, AZ 85255
33.649308, -111.852055

Saguaro Rib Trail

Tucson, AZ 85735
32.195955, -111.060647

San Juan Trailhead

Alta Trail,
Phoenix, AZ 85339
33.330357, -112.144199

San Pedro Trail

Sierra Vista, AZ 85650
31.550220, -110.143389

San Tan Trail

Queen Creek, AZ 85142
33.167221, -111.636283

Sarasota Trailhead

S Sarasota Blvd,
Tucson, AZ 85713
32.190090, -111.076268

Saulsberry Trail Trailhead

13453 Saulsberry Trail,
Pearce, AZ 85625
31.865642, -109.338585

Scenic Trail

McDowell, AZ 85264
33.700983, -111.718647

Secret Trail

Phoenix, AZ 85042
33.337468, -112.015913

Shoreline Trail

Lake Havasu City, AZ 86403
34.461850, -114.340355

Sidewinder {trail}

Phoenix, AZ 85048
33.327170, -112.019748

Siphon Draw Shortcut Trailhead

N Holmes Road,
AZ 85119
33.451573, -111.478228

Sky Islands Traverse

San Simon, AZ 85632
31.916582, -109.268481

Sky Islands Traverse
Cochise, AZ 85606
31.922167, -109.967230

Sky Islands Traverse
Sierra Vista, AZ 85635
31.626823, -110.173794

Sky Islands Traverse
Mt Lemmon, AZ 85619
32.428235, -110.755907

Soldier's Trail

Flagstaff, AZ 86004
35.139974, -111.687693

Stargazer Trail

Queen Creek,
AZ 85142
33.161769, -111.644923

Starr Pass Trail

Tucson, AZ 85746
32.184595, -111.071301

Stoneman Wash Trail

Scottsdale, AZ 85262
33.681017, -111.727019

Sunrise Trail

Scottsdale, AZ 85259
33.602579, -111.810389

Sunrise Trail View area,
Scottsdale, AZ 85259
33.605074, -111.778008

Sunset Vista Trail

Picacho, AZ 85141
32.647453, -111.429211

Taliesin Trail

Scottsdale, AZ 85255
33.617383, -111.851750

Telegraph Pass Entrance

Phoenix, AZ 85042
33.317625, -112.066629

The Wave Trail

Arizona
36.996182, -112.005328

Tom's Thumb Trail

Scottsdale, AZ 85255
33.692947, -111.802533

Tonto Tank Trail

Fountain Hills, AZ 85268
33.678233, -111.728980

Tortoise Trail

Fort McDowell, AZ 85264
33.689913, -111.719166

Trail 28

Dewey, AZ 86327
34.683600, -112.170257

Trail 533

Dewey, AZ 86327
34.677475, -112.17386

Tucson Area Trails

Desert and mountains surround Tucson Arizona and this coupled with
great year round weather makes for great hiking and horseback riding.

The following are some of the trails in the Tucson area, some of which are shown elsewhere in this camping and trail guide.

36th Street Trail
Tucson, AZ 85713
32.195710, -111.048856

Babad Do'ag Trail
Tucson, AZ 85749
32.309276, -110.719359

Bajada Wash Trail
Tucson, AZ 85745
32.271337, -111.209847

Bear Canyon Road Trail
Tucson, AZ 85749
32.302066, -110.802379

Blacketts Ridge Trail
Tucson, AZ 85718
32.318061, -110.807703

Brown Mountain Trail
Tucson, AZ 85743
32.239126, -111.165808

Brown Mountain Trail Parking,
Tucson 85743
32.223732, -111.144599

Bowen Trail
Tucson, AZ 85745
32.215309, -111.052493

Cactus Forest Trail
Tucson, AZ 85748
32.220320, -110.725508

Cactus Wren Trail
Tucson, AZ 85743
32.290967, -111.208195

Cam-Boh Trail
Tucson, AZ 85745
32.327397, -111.130492

Camino De Oeste Trailhead
Tucson, AZ 85745

32.226547, -111.062872

Cat Mountain Trail
Tucson, AZ 85746
32.189738, -111.065292

Cheops Trail
Tucson, AZ 85745
32.220168, -111.107343

Cougar Trail
Tucson, AZ
32.222361, -111.132521

Cougar Trail Parking
Tucson, AZ
32.240959, -111.159316

David Yetman West Trailhead
Tucson, AZ 85735
32.217308, -111.102875

Dobe Wash Trail
Tucson, AZ 85745
32.278763, -111.176163

Encinas Trail
Tucson, AZ 85743
32.306193, -111.216456

Explorer Trail
Tucson, AZ 85746
32.184921, -111.019922

Finger Rock (Canyon) Trail
32.337362,-110.9098

Finger Rock Spring
32.348682,-110.903501

Finger Rock Trail –
Mt. Kimball summit area
32.376625,-110.879366

Gates Pass Trail Parking,
Tucson, AZ
32.223265, -111.101462

Gates Pass Trail at Kinney Road
32.221801, -111.132341

Gould Mine Trail,
Tucson, AZ 85745
32.247538, -111.168075

Hidden Canyon Trail,
Tucson, AZ 85745
32.216943, -111.050015

Hugh Norris Trail,
Tucson, AZ 85745
32.271454, -111.203139

Ironwood Forest Trail
Tucson, AZ 85745
32.325199, -111.135273

King Canyon Trailhead,
Tucson, AZ 85745
32.246612, -111.166876

Loma Verde
Tucson, AZ 85748
32.203392, -110.709865

Manville Trail
Tucson, AZ 85743
32.306112, -111.216563

Mesquite Trail
Tucson, AZ 85748
32.205108, -110.710477

Mica View Trail
Tucson, AZ 85748
32.220524, -110.726249

Mule Deer Trail
Tucson, AZ 85745
32.323456, -111.135988

Phoneline Trail, Tucson
Tucson, AZ 85750
32.311442, -110.810125

Pima Canyon / Iris DeWhirst Trail
Tucson, AZ 85718
32.353323, -110.948079

Pontatoc Canyon (Ridge) Trail
32.336876,-110.9099

Pontatoc Canyon (Ridge) Trail - end
32.347063,-110.8870

Richard E. Genser Starr Pass Trailhead
S Ave Del Correcaminos,
Tucson, AZ 85713
32.205370, -111.046654

Richard Genser Starr Pass Trail
Tucson, AZ 85745
32.199939, -111.038541

Richard Genser Starr Pass Trail
Tucson, AZ 85745
32.199215, -111.044351

Ringtail Trail
Tucson, AZ 85745
32.326279, -111.131722

Rock Wren Trail
Tucson, AZ 85735
32.202778, -111.058102

Rock Wren Trail
Tucson, AZ 85713
32.200937, -111.045962

Saguaro Rib Trail
Tucson, AZ 85735
32.197060, -111.060700

Sendero Esperanza Trail
Tucson, AZ 85745
32.256502, -111.158439

Sendero Esperanza Trail Parking
Tucson, AZ 85745
32.284683, -111.167270

Shantz Trail
Tucson, AZ 85748
32.220597, -110.726109

Starr Pass Trail
Tucson, AZ 85713
32.184596, -111.071286

Tanque Verde Ridge Trail
Tucson, AZ 85748

32.165578, -110.723922

Wild Horse Canyon Trail
Tucson, AZ 85748
32.235334, -110.689448

Yetman Trail (Camino de Oeste Trailhead)
Tucson, AZ 85745
32.226300, -111.062800

Yetman Trail
Tucson, AZ 85735
32.198953, -111.087852

Yetman Trail
Tucson, AZ 85735
32.202819, -111.058123

Yetman Trail
Tucson, AZ 85745
32.218055, -111.064695

End Tucson, Arizona Trails

Turkey Springs Trail

Payson, AZ 85541
34.408188, -111.378550

Turkey Springs Trail

Pine, AZ 85544
34.420755, -111.405183

Upper Green Mountain Trailhead

Mt Lemmon Hwy, AZ 85619
32.397852, -110.689419

W Webber Trail

Payson, AZ 85541
34.409388, -111.386805

Wagner Trail
Scottsdale, AZ 85262
33.698604, -111.743340

Warpaint S {trail}
Phoenix, AZ 85042
33.331192, -112.024508

White Rock Canyon {Trail}
Willow Beach, AZ 86445
35.980182, -114.697315

Willow Canyon Trailhead
Apache Trail,
Mesa, AZ 85215
33.500860, -111.462616

Willow Dells Slickrock Trail Loop
Arizona 86301
34.610113, -112.439141

Windgate Pass Trail
Scottsdale, AZ 85255
33.666062, -111.834917

Woods Canyon Trail
Sedona, AZ 86351
34.756485, -111.763621

Yetman Trail

(Camino de Oeste Trailhead)
Tucson, AZ 85745
32.226300, -111.062800

Colorado Campgrounds, RV Parks, and Hiking Trails

Colorado Campgrounds & RV Parks

5 Branches Camper Park
4677 Co Road 501A
Bayfield, CO 81122
37.405698, -107.531171

Almont Campground
Gunnison, CO 81230
38.655842, -106.855326

Arapaho National Wildlife Refuge
953 Co Rd 32 #32,
Walden, CO 80480
40.617668, -106.276892

Arkansas Point Campground
640, Pueblo, CO 81005
38.251541, -104.732410

Arkansas River Rim Campground
33198 US-24,
Buena Vista, CO 81211
38.899817, -106.173322

Arrowhead Point Camping Resort
33975 US-24,

Buena Vista, CO 81211
38.910439, -106.179634

Aspenglen Campground

Estes Park, CO 80517
40.399266, -105.592626

Aspen Trails Campground

19991 Colorado 65,
Cedaredge, CO 81413
38.944061, -107.926100

Backcountry Permit Office

Mills Drive,
Estes Park, CO 80517
40.365430, -105.558733

Big Creek Campground

Forest Road 121
Cedaredge, CO 81413
39.078442, -107.883944

Black Canyon RV Park & Campground

348 U.S. 50,
Cimarron, CO 81220
38.396149, -107.493873

Blue Creek RV Park

Creede, CO 81130
37.770360, -106.797406

Bookcliff Campground

Loma, CO 81524
39.269062, -108.836993

Burro Bridge Campground

145 West Dolores Road
Dolores, CO 81323
37.486677, -108.592217

Caddis Flats Campgrounds

Placerville, CO 81430
38.027807, -108.091623

Camelot RV Storage LLC

{Not an RV park. There are several RV dealers in this area}
4075 Camelot Circle
Longmont, CO 80504
40.217625, -104.974572

Camp Hale East Fork Campground

Forest Road 7261A
White River National Forest, CO 80461
39.419688, -106.289396

Camp Hale Memorial Campground

Forest Road 7161A
White River National Forest, CO 80461
39.420061, -106.314866

Camping World

6830 Bandley Drive
Fountain, CO 80817
38.732714, -104.738577

Campland RV Park

330 East U.S. Hwy. 24,
Burlington, CO 80807
39.304140, -102.254330

Cañon City RV Campground

3120 E Main Street
Cañon City, CO 81212
38.446555, -105.192170

Capote Campground

Pagosa Springs, CO 81147
37.207523, -107.260326

Carpios Ridge Campground

State Highway 12
Trinidad, CO 81082
37.143925, -104.570188

Carracas Campground

County Road 982,
Arboles, CO 81121
37.006546, -107.416706

Cayton Campground

Ten Peaks Trail
Rico, CO 81332
37.771090, -107.977828

Cedar Creek RV Park

126 Rose Lane

Montrose, CO 81401
38.485091, -107.860430

Chambers Lake Campground

Chambers Lake Colorado 14,
Bellvue, CO 80512
40.597475, -105.851956

Chapman Campground

Frying Pan Road East,
Meredith, CO 81642
39.309530, -106.640877

Chris Park Group Campground

Forest Road 791
Durango, CO 81301
37.519652, -107.805327

Circle C RV

28000 Road T,
Dolores, CO 81323
37.454730, -108.538085

Clear Fork Campground

Crawford, CO 81415
38.679729, -107.596582

Conejos River Campground RV Park

26714 CO-17,
Antonito, CO 81120
37.066995, -106.222536

Cortez / Mesa Verde KOA

27432 U.S. 160
Cortez, CO 81321
37.353043, -108.545614

Cottonwood Campground

Cedaredge, CO 81413
39.071772, -107.961748

Cottonwood Grove Camping Loop

Aurora, CO 80015
39.648708, -104.843411

Country Comfort RV Park

16466 US-34,
Fort Morgan, CO 80701
40.253635, -103.839955

Cozy Comfort RV Park

1501 Central Avenue,
Dolores, CO 81323
37.476146, -108.490319

Crag Crest Campground

Forest Road 121,
Cedaredge, CO 81413
39.049022, -107.937865

Crow Valley Campground

44741 Co Rd 77,
Briggsdale, CO 80611
40.645541, -104.339039

Crowley Lake RV Park

515 S Landing Road
Mammoth Lakes, CA 93546
37.567601, -118.742300

Crystal Meadows Resort & RV Park

Colorado 81434
38.938939, -107.358618

Cutthroat Bay Group Campground

Grand Lake, CO 80446
40.190438, -105.874072

Dakota Campground

Walsenburg, CO 81089
37.645332, -104.790886

Dearhamer Campground

Fryingpan Road,
Basalt, CO 81621
39.360908, -106.738699

Denver Creek Campground

Granby, CO 80446
40.254721, -106.079493

Dexter Point Campground

CO-82,
Twin Lakes, CO 81251
39.092016, -106.323557

Difficult Campground

{Access Road to camp}
Aspen, CO 81611
39.148806, -106.781503

Dolores River Campground and Cabins

18680 CO-145,
Dolores, CO 81323
37.474468, -108.454080

Dolores River Crossing

Gateway, CO 81522
38.452670, -108.861131

Drake Campground

1601 US-34,
Drake, CO 80515
40.432316, -105.340307

Durango KOA Holiday

30090 US-160,
Durango, CO 81303
37.227611, -107.802953

Durango Riverside Resort & RV

13391 County Road 250
Durango, CO 81301
37.454188, -107.801745

Durango RV Park

Open Year Round
5875 U.S. 550
Durango, CO 81303

37.079270, -107.868246

Eagles Nest RV Park

1213 County Road 982
Arboles, CO 81121
37.023645, -107.414823

Echo Canyon Campground

45044 U.S. 50
Cañon City, CO 81212
38.495829, -105.320897

El Monte RV Rentals

5989 Main Street
Louviers, CO 80131
39.482994, -104.997936

Elephant Rock Campground

32201 Co Rd 371
Buena Vista, CO 81211
38.884647, -106.152193

Elk Creek Campground & RV Park

143 County Road 48
Grand Lake, CO 80447
40.255882, -105.841278

Elk Park Trailhead

Woodland Park, CO 80863
38.876282, -105.065470

Erickson Springs Campground

25130 Co Rd 12, Somerset, CO 81434
38.954357, -107.270256

Estes Park Campground at Mary's Lake

2120 Mary's Lake Road
Estes Park, CO 80517
40.347040, -105.532095

Estes Park KOA

2051 Big Thompson Ave,
Estes Park, CO 80517
40.378212, -105.487196

Fireside Cabins and RV Park

6850 US-34,
Loveland, CO 80537
40.417697, -105.177032

Five Star RV Center Inc

12202 Brighton Road
Henderson, CO 80640
39.917417, -104.866311

Fort Collins / Poudre Canyon KOA

6670 N US Highway 287
Laporte, CO 80535
40.663912, -105.186800

Fort Collins KOA Lakeside

1910 Lakeside Resort Lane
Fort Collins, CO 80524
40.614901, -105.107066

Forts RV Park

3015 Lake Avenue,
Pueblo, CO 81004
38.220136, -104.625935

Forts RV Park

3015 Lake Avenue
Pueblo, CO 81004
38.220139, -104.625955

Four Seasons River Inn & RV Park

676 U.S. 50,
Delta, CO 81416
38.751919, -108.069654

Fowler RV Park

E Cranston Avenue
Fowler, CO 81039
38.130456, -104.018638

Freeman Mesa Campground

Basalt, CO 81621
39.362234, -106.777262

Gates of Lodore

Entry road to the Gates of Lodore
{Take country road 10 to first right onto county road 34, and follow it to the Green River Lodore Ranger Station. The Gates of Lodore is the scenic entrance to the Canyon of Lodore, a canyon on the Green River in northwestern Colorado}
40.715302, -108.751461

Graham Creek Campground

San Juan National Forest, Co Road 501A,
Bayfield, CO 81122
37.389890, -107.540905

Grand Junction KOA

2819 U.S. 50,
Grand Junction, CO 81503
39.035596, -108.529894

Green Ridge Campground

Grand Lake, CO 80447
40.206415, -105.844986

Grottos Day Use Area

Aspen, CO 81611
39.119544, -106.703644

Haviland Lake Campground

Forest Road 671
Durango, CO 81301
37.533617, -107.807579

Heart of Rockies Campground

Salida, CO 81201
38.536661, -106.175406

Hermits Rest Picnic Area

Cimarron, CO 81220
38.463579, -107.518697

High Country RV Park

218 W Main Street
Naturita, CO 81422
38.217860, -108.571667

Highlander RV Campground

1245 Co Rd 30,
Lake City, CO 81235
37.986487, -107.294093

Highlander RV Campground

(Access Road to Highlander RV Campground and Lake San Cristobal)
Gunnison Ave
Lake City, CO 81235
38.000477, -107.298871

Historic Arkansas Riverwalk of Pueblo

101 South Union Avenue,
Pueblo, CO 81003,
38.265975,-104.61317

Holiday RV

10132 U.S. 50,
Poncha Springs, CO 81242
38.515404, -106.077273

Island Acres Campground

Palisade, CO 81526
39.168498, -108.299723

Island Lake Campground

Forest Road 116,
Cedaredge, CO 81418

39.029859, -108.009213

Jumbo Campground

Colorado 65, Mesa, CO 81643
39.053574, -108.093775

Junction West RV Park

793 22 Road
Grand Junction, CO 81505
39.120110, -108.645624

Kelly Flats Campground

Livermore, CO 80536
40.682472, -105.483901

Kiser Creek Campground

Cedaredge, CO 81413
39.037551, -107.947853

KOA Kampgrounds

27432 U.S. 160
Cortez, CO 81321
37.349649, -108.547206

KOA Kampgrounds

U.S. 50
Cotopaxi, CO 81223
38.378967, -105.667146

La Junta KOA

26680 U.S. 50
La Junta, CO 81050

37.998891, -103.588985

La Veta RV Park
Colorado 81055
37.513527, -105.011564

Lake Fork Campground
Gunnison, CO 81230
38.455020, -107.323116

Lake Granby RV Park
8872-8776 US-34
Granby, CO 80446
40.181802, -105.891450

Limon KOA Journey
575 Colorado Ave,
Limon, CO 80828
39.266186, -103.675019

Lincoln Creek Dispersed Campground
Lincoln Creek Rd,
Buena Vista, CO 81211
39.116991, -106.695836

Little Bear Campground
Forest Road 116,
Cedaredge, CO 81413
39.034453, -107.998901

Little Mattie Campground
Basalt, CO 81621

39.376776, -106.807473

Little Maud Campground

Sporis Ranger District,
Basalt, CO 81621
39.376677, -106.813890

Lost Man Campground

Aspen, CO 81611
39.121671, -106.625037

Lower Beaver Campground

34477-35387 CO-145,
Placerville, CO 81430
38.111398, -108.189810

Manor RV Park

815 Riverside Dr,
Estes Park, CO 80517
40.362513, -105.538989

Marshall Park Campground

{On the Rio Grande River}
Creede, CO 81130
37.790571, -106.981659

Mary's Lake Campground

2120 Mary's Lake Road
Estes Park, CO 80517
40.347050, -105.532126

Matterhorn Campground

Priest Lake Road
Ophir, CO 81426
37.844744, -107.881117

Mesa Campground

36128 U.S. 50,
Gunnison, CO 81230
38.522072, -106.990650

Mesa Creek Campground

Crawford, CO 81415
38.474996, -107.522658

Middle Mountain Campground

San Juan National Forest, Forest Rd 603,
Bayfield, CO 81122
37.410136, -107.536830

Mix Lake Campground

Del Norte, CO 81132
37.357884, -106.542690

Mogote Campground

Antonito, CO 81120
37.064766, -106.235034

Molas Lake Park & Campground Entry Road

U.S. 550,
Silverton, CO 81433

{US-550 is known as the *Million Dollar Highway* in this area - There are
several campgrounds in the area that border Mineral Creek}

37.752402,-107.682989

Monument RV Park

607 Colorado 340
Fruita, CO 81521
39.149349, -108.736858

Mountain Park Campground

Bellvue, CO 80512
40.682480, -105.467492

Mountain View RV Resort

45374-45434 W U.S. 50,
Cañon City, CO 81212
38.496277, -105.310187

Mt Princeton RV Park

30380 Co Rd 383
Buena Vista, CO 81211
38.860420, -106.140927

Municipal Campground

Campground Road,
Brush, CO 80723
40.249057, -103.623382

North Canyon Campground

San Juan National Forest,
Bayfield, CO 81122
37.393737, -107.539034

North Park / Gould / Walden KOA

53337 Colorado 14,
Walden, CO 80480
40.553382, -106.036974

Old Timers Day Use Area

Forest Rd 603,
Bayfield, CO 81122
37.376975, -107.560525

Outpost RV Park

1800 Central Ave
Dolores, CO 81323
37.475438, -108.487755

Parry Peak Campground

Leadville, CO 80461
39.067129, -106.409502

Pepper Pod Campground

{Small RV campground}
450 5th Avenue
Hudson, CO 80642
40.071302, -104.646857

Piedmont Campground

Trinidad, CO 81082
37.141416, -104.544338

Pine Point Campground

San Juan National Forest,
Bayfield, CO 81122
37.400106, -107.535215

Pleasant Valley RV Park

0018 County Road 47,
Howard, CO 81233
38.431201, -105.811625

Pony Express & RV Park

20821 Co Rd 28,
Julesburg, CO 80737
40.966366, -102.252890

Pony Express & RV Park

20821 Co Rd 28,
Julesburg, CO 80737
40.966354, -102.252881

Priest Gulch Campground & RV

27646 CO-145,
Dolores, CO 81323
37.584622, -108.162488

Priest Lake Campground

Priest Lake Road,
Telluride, CO 81435
37.834884, -107.880328

Prospector Campground

Dillon, CO 80435
39.600926, -106.040203

Prospectors RV Resort at Royal

43595 W U.S. 50,
Cañon City, CO 81212
38.498493, -105.348764

Pueblo South / Colorado City KOA

9040 Interstate 25
Pueblo, CO 81004
37.958599, -104.797327

Railroad Bridge Campground

33827 Co Rd 371,
Buena Vista, CO 81211
38.923637, -106.169274

Riverbend Campground LLC

1520 U.S. 34
Loveland, CO 80537
40.429575, -105.324829

Riverview RV Park

2444 River Rim Road,
Loveland, CO 80537
40.415842, -105.188405

Rosa Campground

Arboles, CO 81121
37.007543, -107.410994

Royal Gorge / Canon City KOA

559 Co Rd 3A,
Cañon City, CO 81212
38.489361, -105.330966

Royal View Campground

43590 W U.S. 50,

Cañon City, CO 81212
38.494324, -105.349917

RV Campground

330 Colorado 96,(mailing/office)
322 Colorado 96,
Sheridan Lake, CO 81071
38.465753, -102.289974

Saddlehorn Campground

Grand Junction, CO 81507
39.104551, -108.732861

Sawmill Gulch Campground

Granby, CO 80446
40.200999, -106.035270

Seven Pines Campground & Cabin

2137 US-34,
Drake, CO 80515
40.408498, -105.413107

Shady Creek RV Park

205 N Grand Mesa Drive,
Cedaredge, CO 81413
38.901938, -107.923290

Sky Ute Fairgrounds & RV Park

200 CO-151,
Ignacio, CO 81137
37.112938, -107.630153

Silverton Lakes Campground

2100 Kendall Street
Silverton, CO 81433
37.816959, -107.653331

Sleeping Elephant Campground

Bellvue, CO 80512
40.682755, -105.773340

Slumgullion Pass Campground

{Access Road}
Lake City, CO 81235
37.984715, -107.223093

Snowy Peaks RV Park & Rentals

30430 US-24,
Buena Vista, CO 81211
38.861765, -106.146113

South Fork {Rio Grande} Alpine Trails RV Park

111 Wharton Drive
South Fork, CO 81154
37.671807, -106.643084

South Shore Campground

Trinidad, CO 81082
37.134148, -104.557635

Sportsman's RV Park {US-287

5385 U.S. 50 Scenic,
Lamar, CO 81052
38.112373, -102.660232

Spruce Grove Campground

Colorado 65,
Eckert, CO 81418
39.049047, -108.079571

Spruce Lake RV Park

1023-1039 Mary's Lake Road
Estes Park, CO 80517
40.362430, -105.543375

Stillwater Campground

8590 U.S. 34
Granby, CO 80446
40.180066, -105.888883

Sugarbush Campground and Country Store

9229 U.S. 50
Howard, CO 81233
38.432558, -105.833302

Summit RV Park

9800 Santa Fe Trail
Trinidad, CO 81082
37.130077, -104.519690

Sunshine Campground

Telluride, CO 81435
37.889487, -107.890080

Tarpley RV

25871 U.S. 160
Durango, CO 81301
37.231068, -107.862062

Telluride Town Park Campground

Ophir, CO 81426
37.933650, -107.804593

The Forks Campground

Dolores, CO 81323
37.587787, -108.357864

The Starlite Campground

30 Co Rd 3A,
Cañon City, CO 81212
38.495052, -105.327281

Tiffany Campground

1526 County Road 982,
Arboles, CO 81121
37.004224, -107.418630

Timber Creek Campground

Grand Lake, CO 80447
40.379169, -105.850196

Titan RV Storage

7243 W Titan Road
Littleton, CO 80125
39.508486, -105.023266

Tom Bennett Campground

Bellvue, CO 80512
40.575689, -105.584313

Twin Peaks Campground

Buena Vista, CO 81211
39.067026, -106.421174

United Campgrounds of Durango

1322 Animas View Drive
Durango, CO 81301
37.319754, -107.851197

Ute Creek RV Park

071 5th Avenue,
Fort Garland, CO 81133
37.429374, -105.440266

Vallecito Campground

{Trailhead for Vallecito Creek Trail}
Bayfield, CO 81122
37.477595, -107.546933

Valley Mobile RV Park

30620 US-24,
Buena Vista, CO 81211
38.862907, -106.145886

Walks Camp Park

Limon, CO 80828
39.427833, -103.571175

Ward Lake Campground

Forest Road 121,
Cedaredge, CO 81413
39.036642, -107.984414

Weller Campground

31035 CO-82,
Aspen, CO 81611
39.121330, -106.720549

White Star Campground

Twin Lakes, CO 81251
39.089961, -106.365566

Willow Creek Campground

County Road 40
Granby, CO 80446
40.143246, -105.952127

Wupperman Campground

600 Co Rd 33
Lake City, CO 81235
37.963150, -107.290128

Colorado Hiking Trails

Adams Fork Conejos River Trail

{Continental Divide Trail access point}
Pagosa Springs, CO 81147
37.333920, -106.695145

Alpine Ridge Trail

Estes Park, CO 80517
40.441639, -105.753501

Animas River Crossing - Railroad Stop

{Entry to Chicago Basin Trail}
La Plata County, Colorado
37.633518, -107.692836

Animas River Trail

Durango, CO 81303
37.218612, -107.854053

Antelope Trailhead

371 Antelope Drive
Lyons, CO 80540
40.227669, -105.296079

Arkansas Riverwalk Trail

Cañon City, CO 81212
38.437619, -105.239963

Barr Trail

Cascade, CO 80809
38.840488, -105.041968

Bear Creek Trail

Wasatch Trail,
Ophir, CO 81426
37.932986, -107.810383

Bear Creek Trail - Highline Trail

San Juan National Forest,
Hesperus, CO 81326}
~37.456771,-108.029895

Booth Falls Trailhead

3035 Booth Falls Rd,
Vail, CO 81657
39.650775, -106.321046

Bowen Trail

Grand Lake, CO 80447
40.329226, -105.865757

Butlers' Trail, Continental Divide

Henderson Mine Road,
Arapaho National Forest,
Parshall, CO 80468
~ 39.770176,-105.854162

Chatfield Lake Walking and Biking Path

Littleton, CO 80128
39.552066, -105.047368

Cherry Creek Trail

Aurora, CO 80016
39.625483, -104.845919

Chicago Basin Trail

{Extension of Columbine Lake Shortcut Trail
Bayfield, CO 81122
37.603454, -107.609972

Chicago Basin Trail {Animas River - RR station}
Durango, CO 81301
37.633330, -107.692497

Clifton Nature Park Colorado River Trail

Clifton, CO 81520
39.062660, -108.450607

Colorado Trail

{Continental Divide Trail access point}
Silverton, CO 81433
37.718397, -107.536117

Colorado Trail - Highline Trail
San Juan National Forest,
Hesperus, CO 81326}
~37.456771,-108.029895

Colorado Trail, Colorado Trail Parking - Little Molas Lake,
{Hiking trail, campgrounds, lake}

San Juan National Forest
Durango, CO 81301
37.742765,-107.711624

Colorado Trail
Durango, CO 81301 {Road junction}
37.742542, -107.711834

Colorado Trail,
Durango, CO 81301 {Road junction}
37.718473, -107.891970

Colorado Trail
Silverton, CO 81433 {Road junction}
37.791680, -107.542665

Colorado Trail
Creede, CO 81130 {Road junction}

37.856122, -107.367766

Colorado Trail
Lake City
CO 81235 {Road junction}
37.940942, -107.160187

Colorado Trail
Gunnison, CO 81230 {Road junction}
38.131445, -106.697035

Colorado Trail
Twin Lakes, CO 81251
39.082955, -106.304713

Colorow Trail

New Castle, CO 81647
39.585925, -107.538292

Columbine Lake Shortcut Trail

Bayfield, CO 81122
37.597986, -107.601715

Conejos River Trail

{Continental Divide Trail access point}
Pagosa Springs, CO 81147
37.234155, -106.629447

Continental Divide Trail

Loop Trail,
Creede, CO 81130
37.482912,-106.799855

Continental Divide, Loop Trail, Butlers' Trail

Henderson Mine Road,
Arapaho National Forest,
Parshall, CO 80468

~ 39.770176,-105.854162

Cooper Ranch Trail
Gunnison, CO 81230
38.507822, -107.024645

Cottonwood Creek Trail
Aurora, CO 80016
39.624651, -104.846107

Coyote Valley Trail,
Grand Lake, CO 80447
40.346120, -105.859613

Crews Gulch Trail
Colorado Springs, CO 80911
38.735723, -104.709258

Cross Mountain Trail Head
Durango, CO 81301
37.796328, -107.937586

Crystal Creek Trailhead
Crystal Creek Trail,
Crawford, CO 81415
38.492766, -107.561187

Curecanti Creek Trail
Gunnison, CO 81230
38.453916, -107.414969

Dakota Ridge Trail

{Dinosaur Ridge, Stegosaurus lot}
Golden, CO 80401
39.696564, -105.203583

Deep Creek Trailhead

{South of CO-149 on country road 806 past Airport}
Creede, CO 81130
37.813868, -106.915192

Deer Mountain Trailhead

Estes Park, CO 80517
40.386983, -105.609832

Devil's Backbone Trailhead

Devils Backbone Trail,
Loveland, CO 80538
40.411704, -105.152825

Dinosaur Hill Loop Trail

Grand Junction, CO 81507
39.133077, -108.736281

Doc Holliday's Grave Trailhead

Bennett Ave & 12th St Ditch,
Glenwood Springs, CO 81601
39.541444, -107.321650

Dominguez Canyon Trailhead

Whitewater, CO 81527
38.849617, -108.372376

Echo Canyon Trailhead

12263 CO-82,
Buena Vista, CO 81211
39.071255, -106.470483

El Dorado Lake Trail

{Continental Divide Trail access point}
Silverton, CO 81433
37.714384, -107.534834

Farmers Creek Trail

Monte Vista, CO 81144
37.827942, -106.889086

Farmers Creek Trail Access Road

Creede, CO 81130
37.827936, -106.905090

Fern Lake Trail

Estes Park, CO 80517
40.340159, -105.675434

Forebay Lake Trail

Durango, CO 81301
37.532944, -107.806029

Fountain Creek Regional Trail

Fountain, CO 80817
38.726556, -104.730482

Free Gondola - Telluride Trail

399-301 W San Juan Ave

Telluride, CO 81320
37.936087, -107.813937

Fuchs Ditch Trail

{Continental Divide Trail access point}
Pagosa Springs, CO 81147
37.668913, -107.330402

Glendale Open Space Trail

12300 S Havana Street
Castle Rock, CO 80108
39.491297, -104.870339

Glenwood Canyon Hiking Biking Trail

Glenwood Springs, CO 81601
39.561656, -107.302529

Green Mountain Trail Parking

Grand Lake, CO 80447
40.307390, -105.841415

Green Mountain Trail Parking

Grand Lake, CO 80447
40.282126, -105.838285

Grindstone Trail - Highline Trail

San Juan National Forest,
Hesperus, CO 81326}
~37.456771,-108.029895

Grizzly Creek Trailhead

57051-57105 I-70,

Glenwood Springs, CO 81601
39.561054, -107.249803

Hazel Lake Trail

Bayfield, CO 81122
37.584364, -107.530855

Hazel Lake Trail Shortcut
Bayfield, CO 81122
37.605850, -107.607306

Hermit's Rest Trail

Cimarron, CO 81220
38.463472, -107.519300

Hickory Trail

Fort Collins, CO 80521
40.595151, -105.078294

Highland Mary Lake Trail

Silverton, CO 81433
37.751362, -107.577590

Highline Trail

{Grindstone Trail, Bear Creek Trail, Colorado Trail, San Juan National
Forest, Hesperus, CO 81326}
~37.456771,-108.029895

Historic Arkansas Riverwalk of Pueblo

101 S Union Ave,
Pueblo, CO 81003
38.265973, -104.613156

Independence Lake Trailhead

Lost Man Loop Trail,
Aspen, CO 81611
39.124567, -106.581634

Interim Joder Trailhead

7495 N Foothills Hwy,
Boulder, CO 80302
40.110222, -105.282732

Intermann Trail

Manitou Springs, CO 80829
38.857012, -104.928417

Kawuneeche VC Trail Parking

Grand Lake, CO 80447
40.266362, -105.832594

Knight Ridge Trail

Grand Lake, CO 80447
40.130321, -105.766259

Kokopelli Trail

Loma, CO 81524
39.177904, -108.827468

La Plata Gulch Trailhead

CO-82,
Buena Vista, CO 81211
39.067951, -106.505054

Lawn Lake Trail

Estes Park, CO 80517
40.404630, -105.624936

Left Hand Trail

Longmont, CO 80503
40.101922, -105.275606

Little Molas Lake, Colorado Trail, Colorado Trail Parking

{Hiking trail, campgrounds, lake}
San Juan National Forest,
Durango, CO 81301
37.742765,-107.711624

Long's Canyon Trail

Trinidad, CO 81082
37.118368, -104.603685

Loop Trail

Silverton, CO 81433
37.687223, -107.519095

Loop Trail – Salida

Salida, CO 81201
38.497264, -106.326319

Loop Trail, Continental Divide

Henderson Mine Road,
Arapaho National Forest,
Parshall, CO 80468
~ 39.770176,-105.854162

Lost Man Loop Trial

Aspen, CO 81611
39.121861, -106.624476

Moose Goose Nature Trail

Walden, CO 80480
40.616970, -106.293218

New Santa Fe Regional Trail

U.S. Air Force Academy,
CO 80840
38.957845, -104.834761

New Santa Fe Regional Trail
Palmer Lake, CO 80133
39.120979, -104.911815

New Santa Fe Trailhead
Old Denver Road,
Monument, CO 80132
39.057140, -104.858319

Nordic Priest Lake Trail

Matterhorn Drive
Ophir, CO 81426
37.843290, -107.882633

Ojo Caliente Hiking Trailhead

{Entering New Mexico from Colorado}
36.995441,-105.997295

Old Gordon Trail

Grand Junction, CO 81507
39.031687, -108.630652

Onahu Creek Trail

Trail Ridge Road
Grand Lake, CO 80447
40.325939, -105.853409

Palisade Rim Trail Head

Palisade, CO 81526
39.119003, -108.319265

Pikes Peak Greenway Trail

Colorado Springs, CO 80903
38.844873, -104.827618

Pine Creek Trail

{Accessible by boat}
Gunnison, CO 81230
38.453756, -107.357767

Pine Creek Trailhead

{US-50 side of the river}
Gunnison, CO 81230
38.450316, -107.345242

Pine Creek Trailhead

Road 388, Buena Vista, CO 81211
38.999935, -106.230602

Pipeline Trail

Aurora, CO 80016
39.625638, -104.844509

Poudre Trail

Fort Collins, CO
40.595061, -105.078283

Pueblo Trail

Pagosa Springs, CO 81147
37.190160, -107.310128

Railroad Bed Trail

Aurora, CO 80016
39.624651, -104.846107

Road 505 Trailhead

39.2976 -106, Forest Rd 505,
Meredith, CO 81642
39.297419, -106.587604

Rock Creek Trail

Broomfield, CO 80020
39.950626, -105.099443

Round Mountain National Recreation Trail

1211 Big Thompson Road,
Loveland, CO 80537
40.420132, -105.285211

Royal Gorge Trailhead

Colorado 81212
38.465236, -105.308925

Serpents Trail

Grand Junction, CO 81507

39.031922, -108.631078

Smuggler Mountain Trailhead

Co Rd 21,
Aspen, CO 81611
39.191563, -106.808143

Spooks Bottom Lake Trail

Fruita, CO 81521
39.147635, -108.746612

Spring Creek Trailhead

Co Rd 423,
La Veta, CO 81055
37.372048, -105.105893

Spruce Lake Trail

Estes Park, CO 80517
40.340148, -105.675476

Squaw Creek Trail

{Continental Divide Trail access point}
Pagosa Springs, CO 81147
37.602848, -107.215943

Tenderfoot Mountain Trailhead

Tenderfoot Trail Rd,
Dillon, CO 80435
39.635832, -106.036116

Tennessee Pass Trailhead

(Also the access road to Ski Cooper and the Continental Divide Trail}
Leadville, CO 80461

39.362354, -106.311154

Timber Lake Trail

Grand Lake, CO 80447
40.398191, -105.842957

Toll Memorial Trail

Estes Park, CO 80517
40.412641, -105.732977

Trail

Durango, CO 81301
37.532975, -107.805536

Trail Through Time

Mack, CO 81525
39.193619, -109.020029

Uncompahgre Riverway Trail (Montrose Section)

Montrose, CO 81403
38.471646, -107.882984

Upper Beaver Meadows Trailhead

Estes Park, CO 80517
40.372830, -105.614208

Ute Trail

Estes Park, CO 80517
40.393344, -105.695350

Vallecito Creek Trail

{Continental Divide Trail access point}
Silverton, CO 81433
37.687189, -107.519205

Verde Lake Trail

Silverton, CO 81433
37.768965, -107.627107

Warner Point Trail

Crawford, CO 81415}
~ 38.575347,-107.741632

Wasatch Trail

450 S Pine Street,
Telluride, CO 81435
37.934350, -107.811939

Waterfowl Loop Trail

Grand Junction, CO 81507
39.086601, -108.615603

Wedding Canyon Trail

Grand Junction, CO 81507
39.108739, -108.701519

West Spanish Peak Trail

{Ask locals for the trail to the top}
37.375655, -104.993665

Willis Gulch Trailhead

7418-7498 CO-82,

Twin Lakes, CO 81251
39.066988, -106.400632

Wolf Creek Ski Area Trail

{Continental Divide Trail access point}
Pagosa Springs, CO 81147
37.459625, -106.769416

New Mexico Campgrounds, RV Parks, and Hiking Trails

New Mexico Campgrounds & RV Parks

Albuquerque Central KOA

12400 Skyline Rd NE
Albuquerque, NM 87123
35.073072,-106.509009

Access Road to Water Canyon Campgrounds

US-60
Magdalena, NM 87825
34.080586, -107.082992

Agua Piedra Campground

Forest Service Road 708,
Vadito, NM 87579
36.131858, -105.527000

Agua Vista RV Park

20 Cozy Cove Road
Elephant Butte, NM 87935
33.212280, -107.237696

Aguirre Spring Campground

Aguirre Springs Road,

Las Cruces, NM 88011
32.370000, -106.561293

Alamo RV & Truck Center

7023 U.S. 54
Alamogordo, NM 88310
32.952685, -105.970638

Aloha RV Inc

8300 Pan American Freeway
Albuquerque, NM 87113
35.177958, -106.580940

Along the River RV Park,

Campground and Cabins
127 NM-37, Capitan, NM 88316
33.448556, -105.665369

American RV Park

13500 Central Avenue SW
Albuquerque, NM 87121
35.060394, -106.796926

Angel Peak RV Park

6181 U.S. 64,
Bloomfield, NM 87413
36.706014, -108.019936

Arrowhead Motel & RV Park

25999 US-70, Ruidoso, NM 88345
33.311597, -105.640974

Artesia R V Park & Storage

201 W Hermosa Drive
Artesia, NM 88210
32.826853, -104.397572

Aspen Basin Campground

{Ski area}
NM-475, Santa Fe, NM 87506
35.795479, -105.803831

Avalon Lake Campsite

Carlsbad, NM 88220
32.493685, -104.248864

Bear Trap Campground

Magdalena, NM 87825
33.883020, -107.514148

Big Tesuque Campground

Santa Fe, NM 87506
35.769220, -105.809184

Bighorn Campground

Elms Rd,
Glenwood, NM 88039
33.324081, -108.882770

Black Canyon Campground

704 Hyde Park Road,
Santa Fe, NM 87501
35.727850, -105.839549

Bottomless Lakes Park Campground

18 Park Service Road,
Roswell, NM 88203
33.316477, -104.330831

Bottomless Lakes State Park

545 Bottomless Lakes Road,
Roswell, NM 88203
33.338275, -104.334746

Caballo Lake R.V. Park

14279 NM-187, Caballo, NM 87931
32.918855, -107.317096

Cactus Patch Campground

Las Cruces, NM 88007
32.493129, -106.919553

Cactus RV Park

1316 E Tucumcari Blvd.,
Tucumcari, NM 88401
35.171717, -103.710407

Camp Davis

HC 69 Box 20,
Rociada, NM 87742
35.832274, -105.420839

Camp Washington Ranch

18 Rattlesnake Springs Road,
Carlsbad, NM 88220
32.110342, -104.458975

Camping Navajo Dam

Navajo Dam, NM 87419
36.822421, -107.616436

Camping World of Albuquerque

14303 Central Ave NW
Albuquerque, NM 87121
35.061565, -106.807874

Capulin Camp & RV Park

7 Santa Fe Avenue
Capulin, NM 88414
36.740220, -103.994119

Carlsbad KOA 2 - Holiday

2 Manthei Road,
Carlsbad, NM 88220
32.586403, -104.416163

Carlsbad RV Park & Campground

4301 National Parks Hwy,
Carlsbad, NM 88220
32.368394, -104.236023

Casey's Socorro RV Park

1101 New Mexico 1,
Socorro, NM 87801
34.041810, -106.894021

Cave Campground

E Well Trail,
Lincoln, NM 88338
33.504730, -105.491295

Cedar Cove RV Park

Highway 195 & Yapple Canyon Road 48 Cedar Cove Road
Elephant Butte, NM 87935
33.203578, -107.236378

Cedar Rail RV Park

46020 Interstate 25,
Raton, NM 87740
36.988827, -104.482338

Circle B RV Park

26514 US-70,
Ruidoso Downs, NM 88346
33.347085, -105.569231

Circle Cross RV Park

1282 Sacramento River Road,
Timberon, NM 88350
32.649196, -105.699197

Clayton KOA

903 South 5th Street
Clayton, NM 88415
36.444745, -103.174265

Comales Campground

Vadito, NM 87579
36.160147, -105.588948

Coronado Campground

106 Monument Road

Bernalillo, NM 87004
35.324576, -106.558581

Cosmic Campground

Glenwood, NM 88039
33.479292, -108.922658

Cottonwood RV & MH Park

918 Inspiration Drive,
Española, NM 87532
36.024676, -106.061420

Desert Oasis RV Park

403 4th Street
Eunice, NM 88231
32.435302, -103.148605

Desert Paradise Mobile Home & RV Park

1090 Hwy 70 W # 14
Alamogordo, NM 88310
32.868296, -105.983076

Devil's Inkwell Campground

New Mexico 88203
33.334954, -104.332952

Eagle Creek RV Resort

159 Ski Run Road,
Alto, NM 88312
33.399018, -105.690000

Eagle Lake Campground & RV Park Entrance

Indian Service Rte 21,
Alto, NM 88312
33.390435, -105.735453

Eagle Nest State Park Campgrounds

GPS 36.533847,-105.264387

East Mountain Auto & RV Repair

1902 Hwy 66
Edgewood, NM 87015
35.064691, -106.198659

El Porvenir Campground

Montezuma, NM 87731
35.710411, -105.411989

Elephant Rock Campground

NM-38,
Red River, NM 87558
36.706059, -105.455661

Empty Saddle RV Park

2500 E Rte 66 Blvd.,
Tucumcari, NM 88401
35.171453, -103.694050

Enchanted Trails RV Park & Trading

PO Street 14305 Central Ave NW
Albuquerque, NM 87121
35.061075, -106.810286

EV Long Campground

Las Vegas, NM 87701
35.698407, -105.421968

Evergreen Mobile Home & RV Park

2200 N Florida Ave # 50
Alamogordo, NM 88310
32.917374, -105.952299

Farmington RV Sales

1603 W Main Street
Farmington, NM 87401
36.731187, -108.230894

Fawn Lakes Campground

Red River, NM 87558
36.707441, -105.449179

Gallo Campground

1808 County Road 7950
Nageezi, NM 87037
36.036361, -107.890646

GCW RV & Self Storage

621 Wright Avenue
Alamogordo, NM 88310
32.853063, -105.975138

Glorieta Christian Camps

11 NM-50,
Glorieta, NM 87535
35.593069, -105.767410

Greasewood Campground

Las Cruces, NM 88007
32.490647, -106.920461

Harper Hill RV & Self Storage

4500 Lomas Street
Farmington, NM 87401
36.741982, -108.269656

Head of the Ditch Campground

US-180, Luna, NM 87824
33.817951, -108.990789

High Desert RV Park

13000 Frontage Road SW
Albuquerque, NM 87121
35.061504, -106.791405

Holy Ghost Campground

Tererro, NM 87573
35.772555, -105.700862

Hopewell Lake Campground

US-64,
Tres Piedras, NM 87577
36.701133, -106.235682

Hyde Memorial Park Main Camp Loop

Santa Fe, NM 87506
35.732597, -105.836754

Isleta Lakes & RV Park

4051 New Mexico 327
Albuquerque, NM 87105
34.945389, -106.674305

Jemez Falls Campground

New Mexico 4
Jemez Springs, NM 87025
35.824049, -106.606254

June Bug Campground

Red River, NM 87558
36.707913, -105.434761

Kay's RV

2107 Hwy 66
Moriarty, NM 87035
35.014603, -106.074156

Kiva RV Park

1416 Hwy 66,
Tucumcari, NM 88401
35.171471, -103.708588

Kiva RV Park & Horse Motel

21 Old Highway 60
Bosque, NM 87006
34.415888, -106.842690

KOA Kampground

1330 S 2nd Street
Raton, NM 87740
36.878691, -104.440364

KOA Campground of Las Vegas

Hcr 73
Las Vegas, NM 87701
35.508205, -105.255889

KOA
76 Romeroville Frontage Road
Las Vegas, NM 87701
35.511130, -105.253035

Las Cruces KOA

814 Weinrich Road
Las Cruces, NM 88007
32.292421, -106.859164

Lazy Dayz RV Park

26520 US-70,
Ruidoso Downs, NM 88346
33.348253, -105.565493

Leisure Mountain RV Park

768 New Mexico 333
Tijeras, NM 87059
35.099804, -106.351374

Lil Abners RV Park

14422 NM-187, Caballo, NM 87931
32.935409, -107.315237

Links Tract Campground

 (recgovnpsdata)
Tererro, NM 87573
35.756738, -105.661376

Little Creek RV Park

290 NM-220, Alto, NM 88312
33.418212, -105.636324

Lowry's RV Center

3510 Highway 180 E
Silver City, NM 88061
32.785705, -108.238022

Mama Bear RV Park

214 Smokey Bear Blvd
Capitan, NM 88316
33.545663, -105.573037

Manzano Mountains State Park

Co Road B062,
Mountainair, NM 87036
34.603394, -106.360985

Mom & Pop RV Park

901 Illinois Avenue
Farmington, NM 87401
36.720270, -108.187200

Mora Inn & RV Park

765 NM-518,
Cleveland, NM 87715
35.984472, -105.363114

Morphy Lake State Park

Mora, NM 87732

35.940614, -105.392408

Mountain High RV Park

991 NM-48,
Alto, NM 88312
33.412162, -105.671388

Mountain Road RV Park

1700 S Mountain Road
Tucumcari, NM 88401
35.154902, -103.701579

Oak Grove Campground

Co Rd 532,
Ruidoso, NM 88345
33.396058, -105.746916

OMG! R.V

5026 N Florida Ave
Alamogordo, NM 88310
32.956646, -105.942783

Palisades RV Park

9201 Central Ave NW
Albuquerque, NM 87121
35.075527, -106.736795

Pecos River RV Park & Store

320 E Greene Street
Carlsbad, NM 88220
32.418150, -104.222954

Pine Ridge Campground

124 Glade Drive,
Ruidoso, NM 88345
33.315794, -105.630851

Rancheros De Santa Fe Campground

736 Old Las Vegas Hwy,
Santa Fe, NM 87505
35.545948, -105.864315

Raton Pass Camp & Cafe

46020 Interstate 25
Raton, NM 87740
36.988373, -104.482081

Red Barn RV Park

2806 E 2nd Street
Roswell, NM 88201
33.394014, -104.482065

Red Canyon Camping

Torreon, NM 87061
34.622161, -106.411923

River Ranch RV Park

26876 US-70,
Ruidoso Downs, NM 88346
33.375007, -105.518563

Riverside RV Park

298 Gavilan Canyon Road,
Ruidoso, NM 88345
33.326675, -105.634187

RJ RV Park

2103 S Broadway Street
Truth or Consequences, NM 87901
33.122274, -107.276652

Roadrunner Campground

1371 E Main Street,
Red River, NM 87558
36.698488, -105.393581

Roadrunner Campground

412 24th Street,
Alamogordo, NM 88310
32.918026, -105.957800

Roadrunner R.V. Park

Ogo Wii Road
Santa Fe, NM 87506
35.880409, -106.013055

Rob Jagger Campground

Lincoln County,
Lincoln, NM 88338
33.514159, -105.510278

Route 66 RV Park

1993 Hwy 66
Edgewood, NM 87015
35.058267, -106.183697

Ruidoso Motorcoach Ranch

358 NM-220, Alto, NM 88312
33.426549, -105.630724

RV Campground

Santa Fe, NM 87501
35.743178, -105.834466

RV Sales in Moriarty

NM, 2109 Hwy 66
Moriarty, NM 87035
35.014635, -106.074503

Santa Fe KOA Journey

934 Old Las Vegas Hwy,
Santa Fe, NM 87505
35.546619, -105.836635

Santa Fe Trail Marker

GPS 36.522338,-103.003778

Santa Rosa Campground & RV Park

2136 Hwy 66
Santa Rosa, NM 88435
34.946928, -104.662328

Shady Corner RV Park

100 Rio Grande Avenue
Williamsburg, NM 87942
33.117601, -107.289765

Shady Grove RV Park

212 Alamo Street
Alamogordo, NM 88310
32.973880, -105.977887

Silver City RV Park

1304 N Bennett Street
Silver City, NM 88061
32.778756, -108.271876

Slide Group Area Campground

Sunspot, NM 88349
32.789729, -105.820276

Soledad Canyon Day Use Area

Soledad Canyon Road,
Las Cruces, NM 88011
32.304453, -106.593867

Storrie Lake State Park

3 Esequiel C De Baca LN,
Las Vegas, NM 87701
35.656653, -105.232298

Summerlan RV Park

1900 S Cedar Street
Raton, NM 87740
36.881730, -104.431382

Sundowner Mobile Home & RV Park

201 N Airport Drive
Farmington, NM 87401
36.730914, -108.221669

Terrero Campground

New Mexico 87573
35.743607, -105.677709

The Grapevine Campground

East Fork Road
Silver City, NM 88061
33.178444, -108.202733

Tom's RV Park

506 U.S. 60
Socorro, NM 87801
34.051348, -106.900363

Travelers World Campground

Clovis, NM 88101
34.404076, -103.260560

Tres Ritos Scout Camp

Unnamed Road,
Vadito, NM 87579
36.105950, -105.488606

Tucumcari KOA

6299 Quay Road Al
Tucumcari, NM 88401
35.171338, -103.667514

Twin Spruce RV Park & Camp

621 US-70,
Ruidoso, NM 88345

33.310601, -105.639869

Upper Bonito Dispersed Recreation Area Camping
Nogal, NM 88341
33.465347, -105.799698

USA RV Park
2925 Hwy 66
Gallup, NM 87301
35.507266, -108.811638

Ute Lake State Park Camping Area
Logan, NM 88426
35.355502, -103.448569

Vegas RV Park
504 Harris Road,
Las Vegas, NM 87701
35.622644, -105.224762

Villanueva State Park Office
State Road 3, Villanueva, NM 87583
35.265101, -105.334532

Water Canyon Campground
Water Canyon Road,
Magdalena, NM 87825
34.025476, -107.132369

Western Sky's RV Park
16201 Las Alturas Drive
Vado, NM 88072

32.119845, -106.634159

Whites City RV Park

17 Carlsbad Cavern Hwy, Whites City, NM 88268
32.174422, -104.379653

Windmill RV Park

3624 National Parks Hwy
Carlsbad, NM 88220
32.378541, -104.225873

New Mexico Hiking Trails

Alkali Flat Trailhead
Tularosa, NM 88352
32.820562, -106.273120

Antelope Gap Trail
Fort Stanton, NM 88323
33.513660, -105.524844

Apache Point Observatory
US Frequency Surveillance
2001 Apache Point Rd, Sunspot, NM 88349
32.780213, -105.819749

Arroyo de Los Chamisos Trail
Santa Fe, NM 87505
35.652000, -105.965399

Bear Canyon Trailhead
99999 High Desert Street,
Albuquerque, NM 87111
35.145779, -106.482814

Big Ditch Trail
Silver City, NM 88061
32.771385, -108.275273

Boca Negra Canyon Trails
6001 Unser Blvd NW, *Petroglyph National Monument* (PNM),
Albuquerque, NM 87120

{Most people miss this small area of the PNM, it is a great park with a loop trail, somewhat hilly, that has all sorts of Petroglyphs on display, don't miss it.}
GPS 35.160749,-106.719689

Boca Trail

Des Moines, NM 88418
36.781656, -103.976943

Bonito Rio Trails

Lincoln County
New Mexico 88338
33.517565, -105.487837

Box Canyon Trailhead

(recgovnpsdata)
Torreon, NM 87061
34.620121, -106.407241

Brantley Lake Loop trailhead

Artesia, NM 88210
32.564560, -104.381094

Buffalo Soldier Trail

Fort Stanton, NM 88323
33.504983, -105.555016
33.496578, -105.561576

Buffalo Soldier Trail
Las Cruces, NM 88007
32.491737, -106.920346

Bull of the Woods Trail

{Wheeler Peak Trail}

Taos Ski Valley, NM 87525
36.603397, -105.439935

Camp Wilderness Ridge

New Mexico
32.022784, -104.804165

Capulin Volcano National Monument Entry Road

GPS 36.781266,-103.986518

Parking for Lava Flow Trail
36.778147,-103.97959

Parking for Boca Trail,
36.779872,-103.976948

Parking for Crater Rim Trail
36.782497,-103.972238

Parking for Vent Trail,
36.782497,-103.972238

Capulin Volcano Roadside Marker
GPS 36.742388,-103.995488

Capitan Overlook Trail
Capitan, NM 88316
33.505100, -105.555017
33.518809, -105.536445

Carlsbad Cavern Trail

Carlsbad, NM 88220
32.174986, -104.444711

Cedar Crest Trail

Lincoln, NM 88338
33.512676, -105.489228

Cerro Gordo Trailhead (Dale Ball Trails)

Santa Fe, NM 87501
35.686490, -105.895520

Chamisa Trailhead

Santa Fe, NM 87592
35.728369, -105.864597

Chile Canyons Loop Trail 1

Las Cruces, NM 88007
32.370116, -106.868135

Chile Canyons Loop Trail 2

Las Cruces, NM 88007
32.368478, -106.870632

Chupadera Wilderness National Recreation Trail

San Antonio, NM 87832
33.822299, -106.891440

Cimarroncito Trail and Cyphers Mine Camp Access

{Cimarroncito Canyon State Park roadside Marker}
~GPS 36.553631,-105.127659

Continental Divide Trail

Tierra Amarilla, NM 87575
36.719551, -106.256483

Continental Divide Trail

Grants, NM 87020
34.872506, -107.889914

Copper Ave NE Trailhead

Albuquerque, NM 87123
35.079216, -106.484575

Copper Trailhead

15000 Copper Ave NE,
Albuquerque, NM 87123
35.079217, -106.484701

Crater Rim Trail

Des Moines, NM 88418
36.782257, -103.972262

Crater Rim Trail

36.782497,-103.972238

Creosote Trail

Las Cruces, NM 88007
32.490990, -106.918681

Crest Trailhead

Fs 108,
Nogal, NM 88341
33.494475, -105.783952

Crossover Trail

Santa Fe, NM 87506
35.786911, -105.796857

Dale Ball Trails

Santa Fe, NM 87501
35.690404, -105.895939

35.686490, -105.895520

Dam Trail

Las Cruces, NM 88011
32.353382, -106.759697

Dark Canyon Lookout Observation Site

 (recgovnpsdata)
Carlsbad, NM 88220
32.081641, -104.739603

Deer Lake

GPS 36.507222,-105.028911
{Hiking trail to lake}

Deer Valley Trail

Fort Stanton, NM 88323
33.497102, -105.531681

Desafio Trail

Santa Fe, NM 87506
35.790024, -105.800212

Desert Trails

 [Community Park with hiking]
3123-3185 Mission Road
Las Cruces, NM 88011
32.337135, -106.743410

Devisadero Loop Trail 108 Trailhead

Taos, NM 87571
36.376040, -105.547078

Doña Ana Trailhead

Co Rd D053,
Las Cruces, NM 88007
32.427775, -106.851027

Dripping Springs Trail

15000 Dripping Springs Road,
Las Cruces, NM 88011
32.329867, -106.590456

Dune Life Nature Trail

Tularosa, NM 88352
32.793369, -106.212599

East Mesa Trail

Lincoln, NM 88338
33.507661, -105.498489
33.498983, -105.507329

El Camino Real Historic Trail Site

300 East County Road #1598, San Antonio, NM 87832
{El Camino Real is The King's Highway; this one is not the one in California of the same name.}
33.595288, -107.094899

Embudito Trailhead

Trailhead Rd NE,
Albuquerque, NM 87111
35.136040, -106.481968

Enchanted Hills Path {Trail}

Rio Rancho, NM 87144
35.333839, -106.579496

Fort Stanton

104 Kit Carson Road,
Fort Stanton, NM 88323
33.494195, -105.525926

Fort Stanton Equestrian Trail Head

Lincoln, NM 88338
33.514498, -105.510712

Fort Stanton N Trail

Fort Stanton, NM 88323
33.498509, -105.529376

Fort Stanton S Trail

Lincoln, NM 88338
33.492528, -105.511204

Fort Stanton Trail

Fort Stanton, NM 88323
33.513818, -105.511921

Frazer Mountain Trail

Taos Ski Valley, NM 87525
36.602005, -105.435580

Goodnight Loving Trail

Capulin, NM 88414
~36.741200, -103.993504

Goodnight Loving Trail Marker

GPS {unknown at this time - most existing GPS are not correct}

Grand Enchantment

La Luz Trail
Albuquerque, NM 87122
35.191822, -106.479095

Grand View Trail

High Rolls, NM 88325
32.958293, -105.852318

Guadalupe Ridge Trail

Carlsbad, NM 88220
32.181794, -104.521861
32.173954, -104.498820
32.129340, -104.646288

Holy Ghost Trailhead

Holy Ghost Canyon Road,
Tererro, NM 87573
35.767996, -105.698461

Indian Hollow Trailhead

Las Cruces, NM 88011
32.372353, -106.554925

Indian Mesa Trail

Jemez Springs, NM 87025
35.793756, -106.681213

Indian Wells Canyon Trail

Alamogordo, NM 88310
32.917792, -105.924585

Interdune Boardwalk

Dunes Drive,
Tularosa, NM 88352
32.793413, -106.239434

Jacks Creek Trailhead

Tererro, NM 87573
35.834705, -105.654867

Kit Carson Loop Trail

Fort Stanton, NM 88323
33.513853, -105.512053

La Cueva Picnic Area

Las Cruces, NM 88011
32.334617, -106.598799

La Cueva Trail Head (multiple trails)

Las Cruces, NM 88011
32.334923, -106.599585

Lava Flow Trail

Des Moines, NM 88418
36.777811, -103.977650

Long Canyon Trail

Taos Ski Valley, NM 87525
36.603679, -105.441243

Loop Trail

Glenwood, NM 88039
33.388206, -108.475037

Loop Trail
Glenwood, NM 88039
33.423115, -108.498454

Loop Trail,
New Mexico
 33.304427, -108.319425

Loop Trail

Silver City, NM 88061
32.712443, -108.296023

Lower Mogollon Trail

Las Cruces, NM 88007
32.494892, -106.921861

Malachite Trail

{Wheeler Peak Trail}
Taos Ski Valley, NM 87525
36.606431, -105.426368

Michael Emery Trailhead

High Desert St,
Albuquerque, NM 87111
35.145952, -106.482414

Old Guano Road Trail

Carlsbad, NM 88220
32.177231, -104.438190
32.176038, -104.382509

Outlaw Trail

Fort Stanton, NM 88323
33.505056, -105.554881

Paseo del Bosque Trail

1451 Alameda Blvd NW,
Albuquerque, NM 87114
35.197677, -106.640967

Permian Reef Trail

Carlsbad, NM 88220
32.011218, -104.788238

Pershing Trail

Fort Stanton, NM 88323
33.506879, -105.529337

Pine Tree Loop Trail Head

Las Cruces, NM 88011
32.370207, -106.560028

Pino Trailhead

Albuquerque, NM 87111
35.163293, -106.470141

Pino Trail
Cibola National Forest
Albuquerque, NM 87113 {May be a toll}
35.161736, -106.473666

Pino Trail
Elena Gallegos
Grant, NM 87111
35.162923, -106.469987

Playa Trail

Dunes Drive,
Tularosa, NM 88352
32.795643, -106.211607

Pueblo and Mission Ruins Trail

Pecos, NM 87552
35.549838, -105.687709

Rattlesnake Canyon Trailhead

Carlsbad, NM 88220
32.165603, -104.503286

Red Canyon/Spruce Spring Trailhead

Forest Road 422,
Bosque, NM 87006
34.621892, -106.416645

Rinconada Canyon Trail

7601 St Josephs Ave,
Albuquerque, NM 87120
35.127257, -106.725269

Rocotillo Rapids Trail

Las Cruces, NM 88007
32.368026, -106.870654

Salado Canyon Trail

La Luz, NM 88337
32.963094, -105.855485

San Vicente Trail

Silver City, NM
32.765724, -108.274111

Sandia Foothills Embudo Canyon

NM Trailhead
35.099217, -106.480228

Sands Drive Trail

Carlsbad, NM 88220
32.180384, -104.379054
32.199347, -104.395084

Santa Fe Trail

Watrous, NM 87753
35.907552,-105.031368

Slaughter Canyon Cave Trail

Carlsbad, NM 88220
32.110539, -104.562893

Slaughter Canyon Trail

Carlsbad, NM 88220
32.110539, -104.562893

Soledad Canyon Springs Trail

Las Cruces, NM 88011
32.305883, -106.590417

South Boundary Trail

Taos, NM 87571
36.375127, -105.545126

South Domingo Baca Dam Trail

Albuquerque, NM 87122
35.168342, -106.506990

Special Events Area Trail

Santa Fe, NM 87506
35.790133, -105.800232

Tesuque Creek Trail

{Aspen Vista Picnic Ground}
Santa Fe, NM 87506
35.776819, -105.810075

TH Chamisa Trail

208-, 250 Hyde Park Road,
Santa Fe, NM 87501
35.728846, -105.866052

Trail 202

Carlsbad, NM 88220
32.027546, -104.802790

Trail 205

Carlsbad, NM 88220
32.129687, -104.660947

Trail 210

Carlsbad, NM 88220
32.113922, -104.682866

Trail 224

Carlsbad, NM 88220
32.092998, -104.725791

Trail 225

Carlsbad, NM 88220
32.107846, -104.688672

Trail 67

Carlsbad, NM 88220
32.097716, -104.763691

Trail Head

Cerro Gordo Road,
Santa Fe, NM 87501
35.687204, -105.897173

Trestle Trail

Cloudcroft, NM
32.957350, -105.749648

Twining Blue Lake Trail

{Wheeler Peak Trail}
Taos Ski Valley, NM 87525
36.600144, -105.426582

Upper Mogollon Trail

Las Cruces, NM 88007
32.492202, -106.921583

Vent Trail

36.782497,-103.972238

Wheeler Peak Trail

Taos Ski Valley, NM 87525
36.603534, -105.440541

Williams Lake Trail

Taos Ski Valley, NM 87525
36.572499, -105.436634

Winsor Trailhead

Hyde Park Road,
Santa Fe, NM 87501
35.795647, -105.804788
35.795631, -105.804801

Yucca Canyon Trailhead

Carlsbad, NM 88220
32.098273, -104.587355

Zuni Acoma Trailhead

Grants, NM 87020
34.956052, -107.943160

Utah Campgrounds, RV Parks, and Hiking Trails

Utah Campgrounds & RV Parks

Anderson Cove Campground

6702 UT-39,
Huntsville, UT 84317
41.250475, -111.786540

Antelope Valley RV Park

776 W Main Street
Delta, UT 84624
39.351707, -112.592993

Arapeen Campground

Manti, UT 84642
39.208731, -111.667658

Beach Campground Road

Duchesne, UT 84021
40.191189, -110.456295

Bear Lake Marina Campground

Garden City, UT 84028
41.965064, -111.399196

Beaver KOA

1428 Manderfield Road
Beaver, UT 84713
38.294820, -112.639281

Big Bend Campground

Utah 128,
Moab, UT 84532
38.648839, -109.480524

Big Creek Campground

Big Creek Campground Road
Laketown, UT 84038
41.845151, -111.334923

Birch Campground

Laketown, UT 84038
41.845831, -111.344103

Blue Mountain Trading Post and RV Park

1930 S Main Street
Blanding, UT 84511
37.596549, -109.478743

Bonanza RV and Mobile Home Campground

Vernal, UT 84078
40.365411, -109.493787

Botts Campground

Utah 84317
41.277413, -111.657963

Bullfrog Marina (RV park - Campground)

Hwy 276
Lake Powell, UT 84533
37.521060, -110.725422

Butch Cassidy Campground

1050 S State Street,
Salina, UT 84654
38.943664, -111.855625

Cadillac Ranch RV Park

640 U.S. 191
Bluff, UT 84512
37.282774, -109.551051

Camp Atoka

Utah 84317
41.264034, -111.690272

Camp Kiesel

15510 Causey Drive
Huntsville, UT 84317
41.315847, -111.575798

Camp Mia Shalom

225 Forest Road
Fairview, UT 84629
39.676222, -111.261583

Camp Red Cliffe

12891 UT-39
Huntsville, UT 84317
41.292330, -111.623426

Camperworld – Lakeside Park

8850 South 26500 West
Duchesne, UT 84021
40.170699, -110.490100

Camperworld Utah

Garden City, UT 84028
41.986372, -111.411145

Camperworld-Pine Forest Park

Dutch John, UT 84023
40.885951, -109.462926

Candy Mountain Resort RV Park

Sevier County, UT 84766
38.516755, -112.265812

Canyon Rim Campground

Dutch John, UT 84023
40.884059, -109.547268

Canyons of Escalante RV Park

495 W Main Street
Escalante, UT 84726
37.770291, -111.609646

Carmel Campground

FR193 Manila, UT 84046
40.930743, -109.731342

Castle Valley Mobile Park & RV

405 N 300 W #101

Ferron, UT 84523
39.091649, -111.138622

Cedar Springs Campground

FR392 Dutch John, UT 84023
40.908487, -109.451024

Cemetery Point Picnic Ground

Huntsville, UT 84317
41.263274, -111.804194

Cherokee Springs Golf & RV Resort

Bryce Woodland Estates Road
Hatch, UT 84735
37.558474, -112.454248

Chokecherry Campground

Deer Creek State Park
Chokecherry Campground Road
Wallsburg, UT 84082
40.411399, -111.503255

Circleville RV Park

85 U.S. 89
Circleville, UT 84723
38.170591, -112.278405

Coal Pit Wash Campsite

 Hurricane, UT 84737
37.215851, -113.078216

Cobble Creek Campground

Huntsville, UT 84317
41.293197, -111.659020

Cottonwood Campground

Laketown, UT 84038
41.845799, -111.339790

Cottonwood Campground

Cottonwood Campground Road
Peoa, UT 84061
40.753326, -111.372799

Crandall Campground

Utah 302
Peoa, UT 84061
40.764969, -111.382153

Crandall Cove Group Campground

Peoa, UT 84061
40.765924, -111.381979

Crazy Horse RV Campark

625 E 300 S
Kanab, UT 84741
37.043913, -112.516371

Deer Creek Campground

Wallsburg, UT 84082
40.397283, -111.537892

Deer Creek State Park- Lower Provo River Area

8950 Lower Deer Creek Road
Heber City, UT 84032
40.401212, -111.530818

Dewey Bridge Campground

Dewey Bridge Campground Road
Moab, UT 84532
38.810896, -109.307940

Drinks Canyon Campground

Utah 128,
Moab, UT 84532
38.633979, -109.485076

Duck Creek Campground

Dixie National Forest, FR056
Duck Creek Village, UT 84762
37.520154, -112.697619

Dutch John Draw Group Campground

Forest Road 695
Dutch John, UT 84023
40.934473, -109.424089

Eagles Campground

Eagles Drive,
Huntsville, UT 84317
41.263871, -111.694456

Fillmore KOA,

410 W 900 S Street
Fillmore, UT 84631

38.949061, -112.335333

Firefighters Memorial Campground
FR195
Dutch John, UT 84023
40.892871, -109.454862

Flaming Gorge KOA Camping Resort
320 Utah 43   Manila, UT 84046
40.988603, -109.730417

Forest Road 0208 - Oowah Campground
{Access to Mt. Peale, South Mountain, Castle Mountain, Mt Waas, Manns
Peak, Oowah campground}
GPS 38.343091,-109.207395

Forks of Huntington Campground
Forest Road 0058
Huntington, UT 84528
39.501656, -111.162565

Freedom Ford & Freedom RV
396 S Main Street
Gunnison, UT 84634
39.149460 -111.818882

Glendale East Campground,
Forest Road 531
Dutch John, UT 84023
40.881268, -109.455768

Goose Island Campground

Utah 128, Utah 84532
38.610895, -109.558114

Gooseberry Reservoir Campground

Forest Road 0124
Fairview, UT 84629
39.711724, -111.293854

Grandstaff Campground

Utah 128
Utah 84532
38.611989, -109.532888

Green River Campground

UT-149
Jensen, UT 84035
40.421326, -109.244226

Green River Campground

Green River, UT 84525
38.988020, -110.156343

Green River KOA

Green River, UT 84525
38.991487, -110.140969

Greendale Campground

Forest Road 187
Dutch John, UT 84023
40.882647, -109.461002

Greens Lake Campground

Ashley National Forest
Dutch John, UT 84023
40.872856, -109.539340

Hal Canyon Campground

Moab Utah 128, Utah 84532
38.640926, -109.477404

Hillside Palms RV & Mobile Home

215 N 600 E.,
St George, UT 84770
37.111339, -113.570213

Hitch-N-Post RV Park

196 E 300 S
Kanab, UT 84741
37.042904, -112.524322

Hittle Bottom Campground

Hittle Bottom Campground Road
Moab, UT 84532
38.759880, -109.324773

Honeycomb Rock Campground

Enterprise Utah
37.517995, -113.856654

Hyrum State Park Campground

Hyrum, UT 84319
41.627281, -111.867490

Indian Bay Campground

Indian Bay Campground Road
Duchesne, UT 84021
40.178568, -110.456550

Jefferson Hunt Campground

905 S 7450 E,
Huntsville, UT 84317
41.249351, -111.767882

Juniper Campground

Juniper Campground Road
Peoa, UT 84061
40.782645, -111.393775

Kanab RV Corral

483 S 100 E
Kanab, UT 84741
37.039736, -112.525290

Leeds RV Park & Motel

97 South Valley Road
Leeds, UT 84746
37.233081, -113.362255

Little Bear Group Campground

Forest Road 3248,
Huntington, UT 84528
39.446745, -111.138487

Lizzie & Charlie's RV / ATV Park

99 S Main Street
Marysvale, UT 84750

38.448387, -112.228030

Lodge Pole Campground
Wallsburg, UT 84082
40.312459, -111.259800

Lower Little Bear Campground
Utah 31
Huntington, UT 84528
39.443294, -111.136225

Lower Meadows Campground
Uinta Wasatch Cache National Forest
UT-39
Huntsville, UT 84317
41.286920, -111.644058

Lower Onion Creek Campground
Fisher Towers Road, Utah 84532
38.737231, -109.359386

Lucerne Campground
Manila, UT 84046
40.983980, -109.592222

Magpie Campground
FR 20079,
Huntsville, UT 84317
41.270721, -111.665825

McArthur's Temple View RV Resort
975 S Main Street

St George, UT 84770
37.091394, -113.582142

McHenry Campground

Utah 319
Heber City, UT 84032
40.617972, -111.432282

Meadows Campground

Huntsville, UT 84317
41.286367, -111.644668

Millsite State Park Campground

Ferron, UT 84523
39.093283, -111.194477

Moab KOA

3225 U.S. 191
Moab, UT 84532
38.524347, -109.495925

Monte Cristo Campground

FR 20064
Woodruff, UT 84086
41.463789, -111.497618

Monument Valley Campground

100 Navajo Drive
Oljato-Monument Valley, UT 84536
37.006678, -110.193537

Mount Ogden Stake Camp

UT-39,
Huntsville, UT 84317
41.280326, -111.656948

Mountain View Campground Road

Duchesne, UT 84021
40.189015, -110.452068

Mustang Ridge Campground

FR395
Dutch John, UT 84023
40.926937, -109.440193

North Campground - Bryce

Bryce, UT 84764
37.635238, -112.166906

North Eden Camp Ground

N Eden Campground
Laketown, UT 84038
41.999889, -111.261566

Oak Grove Campground

Oak Grove Campground Road
Moab, UT 84532
38.643603, -109.476538

Old Folks Flat Group Campground

Forest Road 0059
Huntington, UT 84528
39.539252, -111.158923

Panguitch KOA

555 S Main Street
Panguitch, UT 84759
37.814548, -112.434692

Perception Park Campground

12566 UT-39 Scenic, Huntsville, UT 84317
41.289732, -111.640663

Ponderosa Grove Campground

Kanab, UT 84741
37.088642, -112.672980

Rabbit Gulch Campground

Duchesne, UT 84021
40.179785, -110.494806

Red Canyon Campground

Dutch John, UT 84023
40.889575, -109.559162

Retrailia RV Resorts - Lakeside Park

8850 S 26500 W
Duchesne, UT 84021
40.171127, -110.490923

Richfield KOA

590 W 600 S
Richfield, UT 84701
38.759903, -112.095467

River Bend Campground

Utah 31
Huntington, UT 84528
39.439086, -111.134264

Riverside Campground

Riverside Campground Road
Peoa, UT 84017
40.791432, -111.405424

Riverside Oasis Campground

1871 N Hwy 191
Moab, UT 84532
38.605983, -109.582300

Permanently Closed as of Jan 2018

Ruby's Inn RV Park

Bryce, UT 84764
37.668180, -112.158152

S Eden Campground

Laketown, UT 84038
41.931314, -111.283071

Saint George RV Park Campground

2100 E Middleton Drive
St George, UT 84770
37.123222, -113.538162

Sand Hollow State Park Campground

Hurricane, UT 84737
37.122447, -113.384911

Sand Hollow State Park Camping/Picnic Area

Hurricane, UT 84737
37.100230, -113.369974

Sand Island Campground

Bluff, Utah
37.260570, -109.617797

Sand Island Campground

Blanding, UT 84511
37.260731, -109.617709

Sandcreek RV Park

540 Utah 24,
Torrey, UT 84775
38.299477, -111.433240

Sandpit Campground

Hurricane, UT 84737
37.100192, -113.369799

Shady Acres RV Park

300-424 N 200 W.
Huntington, UT 84528
39.333151, -110.969091

Shooting Star RV Resort

2020 Utah 12
Escalante, UT 84726
37.775920, -111.636356

Sleeping Bear Campgrounds

Douglas Mesa Road
Mexican Hat, UT 84531
37.061423, -110.096094

Slick Rock Campground

1301 N Hwy 191
Moab, UT 84532
38.594252, -109.567051

Slickrock Country Camp

Moab, UT 84532
38.593943, -109.565326

Snow Canyon Campground

St George, UT 84770
37.203050, -113.640805

Soldier Creek Campground & Recreation Area

Heber City, UT 84032
40.153676, -111.054451

South Campground

Utah 9 {Zion NP}
Springdale, UT 84767
37.203957, -112.983560

South Fork Campground

UT-39,
Huntsville, UT 84317
41.281844, -111.653617

South-Forty RV Park

1170 N. Highway 89
Marysvale, UT 84750
38.460788, -112.232622

Squaw Flat Campground

GPS 38.145358,-109.802685

St. George RV Resort

5800 Old Highway 91
Hurricane, UT 84737
37.205285, -113.392898

Starvation State Park Campground

24220 W 7655 S State Park Road
Duchesne, UT 84021
40.190191, -110.451961

Stateline Campground

Evanston, UT 82930
40.982603, -110.384752

Sunrise Campground

FR102
Garden City, UT 84028
41.918914, -111.460977

Thousand Lakes RV Park

1110 Utah 24,
Torrey, UT 84775
38.301784, -111.445085

Upper Big Bend Campground

Upper Big Bend Campground Road,
Moab, UT 84532
38.649170, -109.488195

Upper Meadows Campground

Uinta Wasatch Cache National Forest, UT-39,
Huntsville, UT 84317
41.290825, -111.635289

Wakara Campground

Manti, UT 84642
39.206139, -111.664630

Watchman Campground

C Loop,
Springdale, UT 84737
37.198124, -112.986509

West Marsh Lake Campground

Uinta Wasatch Cache National Forest
Forest Road 606
Evanston, UT 82930
40.954028, -110.397789

Westside Campground

Hurricane, UT 84737
37.122563, -113.384776

White House Campground

White House Trailhead Road,
Utah 84741
37.079828, -111.889550

Wide Hollow Campground

Escalante, UT 84726
37.787079, -111.631148

Willow Campground

Laketown, UT 84038
41.846710, -111.347257

Willow Creek Campground

Willow Creek Campground Road
Willard, UT 84340
41.418994, -112.054945

Willows Campground

Uinta Wasatch Cache National Forest, UT-39,
Huntsville, UT 84317
41.291507, -111.632939

WillowWind RV Park

1150 W 80 S
Hurricane, UT 84737
37.174995, -113.309167

Wonderland RV Park

44 Utah 12,
Torrey, UT 84775
38.298306, -111.402288

Zion Park RV and Campground

UT-9
Mt Carmel, Kane County, UT 84755

37.236289, -112.855957

Zion West RV Park

175 South Valley Road
Leeds, UT 84746
37.232347, -113.363253

Zion's Gate RV Park

150 North 3700 W.
Hurricane, UT 84737
37.170332, -113.371559

Utah Hiking Trails

Agua Canyon Connecting Trail

Utah
37.520160, -112.248361

Angels Landing Trail

Hurricane, UT 84737
37.274842, -112.950724

Archaeology Trail

Hurricane, UT 84737
37.199920, -112.985711

Arizona Scenic Trail,

{Utah end point}
Marble Canyon, UT 86036
37.001253, -112.034049

Beck Hill Trail

St George, UT 84770
37.156308, -113.622583

Big Fill Loop Trail

Corinne, UT 84307
41.637240, -112.491508

Bonneville Shoreline Trail Parking Lot

Uinta-Wasatch-Cache National Forest
Provo, UT

GPS 40.224185,-111.625514

Box Canyon Trail
Jensen, UT 84035
40.428191, -109.169247

Bridal Veil Falls Trail
{Walk in only}
Provo, UT 84604
40.338967, -111.601861

Bristlecone Loop Trail
Kanab, UT 84741
37.475126, -112.239791

Brooks Nature Trail
St George, UT 84770
37.119192, -113.582796

Butterfly Trail
Snow Canyon Drive
Ivins, UT 84738
37.215745, -113.643627

Butterfly Trail - Snow Canyon Drive
37.230847, -113.633769

Cable Mountain Trail
Springdale, UT 84767
37.257880, -112.924758

Canyon Overlook Trail

Hurricane, UT 84737
37.213361, -112.940706

Cave Spring Trail

GPS 38.157245,-109.751723

Charlie Taylor Water Wheel Trail

Water Street
GPS 39.740417,-105.515862

Chinle Trail

Hurricane, UT 84737
37.171294, -113.029941

Chuckawalla Trail Head

10 N 100 E,
St George, UT 84770
37.137991, -113.604616

Cinder Cone Trail

St George, UT 84770
37.246593, -113.628066

Connector Trail

Virgin, UT 84779
37.340607, -113.113241

Connector Trail

Springdale, UT 84767
37.339557, -113.061910

Continental Divide Trail

Bryce, UT 84764
37.602596, -112.156144

Cottonwood Hills Trail

Washington, UT 84780
37.186754, -113.424358

Cottonwood Trail

Washington, UT 84780
37.184332, -113.415182

Coyote Trail, Utah

37.014214, -111.611868

Curtis Bench Trail

Green River, UT 84525
38.572189,-110.709996

Deer Creek Dam Trailhead

Provo-Jordan River Parkway
Wallsburg, UT 84082
40.405913, -111.533359

Deertrap Mountain Trail

(Stave Trailhead to Cable Mountain Trail and Deertrap Mountain Trail)
W Pine Street,
Mt Carmel, UT 84755
37.267741, -112.899484

Dinosaur Quarry Trail

Jensen, UT 84035

40.438447, -109.307081

Dixie Overlook Trail
St George, UT 84770
37.116358, -113.580082

E Mesa Trail
Springdale, UT 84767
37.296981, -112.900143

East Rim Trail
Orderville, UT 84758
37.251884, -112.877183

East Rim Trail Head
Utah 9
Springdale, UT 84755
37.234251, -112.877493

Emerald Pools Trail
Hurricane, UT 84737
37.260083, -112.951569

Fairyland Loop Trail
Bryce, UT 84764
37.649368, -112.146989

Fairyland Loop Trail
Bryce, UT 84764
37.631934, -112.162639

Forest Trail
Bryce, UT 84764

37.666695, -112.139174

Gemini Bridges Trailhead
GPS 38.65646,-109.67780

Gila Trail Head - Snow Canyon Drive
37.230847, -113.633769

Grand Wash Trailhead
Parking is to the right at GPS 38.278113,-111.192278, the ~ 1.5 mile trail goes to a parking lot at GPS 38.263751,-111.215892, which is accessible from *Scenic Drive* (the one that starts at the *Visitor's Center* at GPS 38.291621,-111.261286), at GPS 38.256102,-111.232651

Grapevine Trail
Washington, UT 84780
37.149567, -113.490541

Halfway Wash Trail
St George, UT 84770
37.138589, -113.612912

Hancock Road
{Turn off to Ponderosa Grove Campground}
Kanab, UT 84741
37.076356, -112.702615

Henrys Fork Trail
Evanston, UT 82930
40.909120, -110.331514

Hickman Natural Bridge Trailhead

Parking is to the left at GPS 38.28861,-111.228595
The walk is about 1 mile round trip

Hiking Trail

Forest Rd 1173
37.661362, -112.158788

Hiking at South Mountain Trail Head

GPS 38.401142,-109.261119

Hog Canyon Trail

Utah 84035
40.430202, -109.172898

Hop Valley Trail

Virgin, UT 84779
37.340307, -113.113177

Indian Canyon Trail

Duchesne, UT 84021
40.157013, -110.405956

Jacob Hamblin Trail

Santa Clara, UT 84765
37.140255, -113.666668

Kolob Arch Trail

{Access from the La Verkin Creek Trail}
New Harmony, UT 84757
37.423780, -113.157748

La Verkin Creek Trail

New Harmony, UT 84757
37.417100, -113.146845

Lee Pass Trailhead

New Harmony, UT 84757
37.452107, -113.191300

Left Fork Trailhead

Washington, UT 84767
37.284654, -113.095859

Loop Trail

Bryce, UT 84764
37.602652, -112.156200

Loop Trail
Bryce, UT 84764
37.561413, -112.231443

Loop Trail
Utah
37.527416, -112.241025

Loop Trail
Utah
37.474979, -112.236782

Lost Creek Falls

{Walk in only}
Provo, UT 84604
40.350011, -111.610725

Moab Canyon Pathway

Moab, UT 84532
38.604059, -109.574665

Navajo Loop Trail

Bryce, UT 84764
37.622597, -112.165734

Negro Bill Canyon

{Parking for Trail}
Moab, UT 84532
38.609776, -109.533572

Northgate Peaks Trail

Springdale, UT 84767
37.340090, -113.059701

Observation Point Trail

Springdale, UT 84767
37.281052, -112.936628

Ogden Canyon Trail Head

Ogden River Parkway
Ogden, UT 84404
41.236979, -111.928121

Ogden River Parkway Trail

Botanical Garden
Ogden, UT 84401
41.235535, -111.953678

Pacheco Trail

Blanding, UT 84511
37.625411, -109.473227

Paria View

{Park and then walk in}
Bryce, UT 84764
37.595253, -112.171103

Pa'rus Trail

Hurricane, UT 84737
37.218126, -112.974096

Petrified Forest Trail

Hurricane, UT 84737
37.192973, -113.052885

Piracy Point

{Walk in only}
Bryce, UT 84764
37.546368, -112.244558

Porcupine Trail Single Track

(Bike Trail that starts at picture spot on Colorado River)
Moab, UT 84532
GPS 38.61205,-109.532179

Prospector Trail

Washington, UT 84780
37.157115, -113.479693

Provo River Parkway Biking and Hiking Trailhead

9 N Carterville Road
Orem, UT 84097
40.314171, -111.655254

Provo River Trail Drinking Fountain

Provo, UT 84604
40.323138, -111.647530

Queens Garden Trail

Bryce, UT 84764
37.628408, -112.162936

Rainbow Gardens Trail Head

Bonneville Shoreline Trail
Ogden, UT 84404
41.235173, -111.930778

Rim Trail

Bryce, UT 84764
37.649338, -112.147053

Rim Trail Parking
Parking for the Rim Trail is at
37.271225,-112.939317.

Rim Trail / Fairland Loop Trail
{Walk in on Rim Trail}
Bryce, UT 84764
37.649159, -112.147385

River Trailhead (North End

Jensen, UT 84035
40.437917, -109.252837

Riverside Walk

Springdale, UT 84767
37.285172, -112.947626

Sand Bench Trail

Hurricane, UT 84737
37.238382, -112.965570

Skull Crack Trailhead

Skull Crack Canyon Road
Huntsville, UT 84317
41.289780, -111.582776

Snow Canyon Drive

{Goes to Gila Trail Head, Butterfly Trail, Snow Canyon State Park,
Petrified Sand Dunes, Snow Canyon Campground}
St George, UT 84770
37.230847, -113.633769

State Canyon Trail Parking Lot

Uinta-Wasatch-Cache National Forest
Provo, UT
GPS 40.224185,-111.625514

Sunrise Point

{Queens Garden Trail}
Bryce, UT 84764
37.628298, -112.162976

Sunset Point

{Navajo Loop Trail / Rim Trail}
Bryce, UT 84764
37.622599, -112.165980

Tanner Bike Trails

2870 E 2850 S,
Salt Lake City, UT 84109

40.710550, -111.809321

Taylor Creek Trail

New Harmony, UT 84757
37.461940, -113.199464

The Gap Trail

St George, UT 84770
37.144182, -113.619607

The 'Living Room' Trail Head

383 Colorow Road,
Salt Lake City, UT 84108
40.759330, -111.821295

The Narrows Bottom Up

UT 84767
37.296662, -112.948257

The Wave Trail

Kanab, Utah 84741
37.019090, -112.024827

Timber Creek Overlook Trail

New Harmony, UT 84757
37.435568, -113.202012

Trailhead to Coldwater Springs Canyon/Old CCC Encampment

Ogden, UT 84403
41.240144, -111.904278

Turtle Wall Trail

St George, UT 84770
37.153521, -113.623044

Watchman Trail

Hurricane, UT 84737
37.201351, -112.986464

West Rim Trail

Hurricane, UT 84737
37.260100, -112.951481

Whiteman Bench Connecting Trail

Bryce, UT 84764
37.564856, -112.237920

Wildcat Canyon Trail

Springdale, UT 84767
37.339839, -113.075656

Zion Hiking Trails in the Park and Area

See the ranger stations for detailed maps and for current weather and flooding conditions; many of these trails are within *Slot Canyons and can become deadly due to flash flooding,* which can be caused by a rain storms miles outside the park.

The Author

The author has traveled to many of the locations listed in this e-book, and found that most people pass by places of interest, including him at one time, without ever knowing the places existed. This prompted him to do the research that led to the compilation of places to visit and stay while camping or hiking, along with the GPS of where each is located.

The listing includes federal, state, and local campgrounds, private and government RV camping parks, and public access hiking trails.

Bill has for nearly a decade either setup and provided tours, or assisted other tour guides on hundreds of tours in the Northeast, West, and the Southwest.

His series of guidebooks include the Philadelphia area, California, Arizona, Colorado, New Mexico, Utah, South Dakota, and other states.

The *RoadSites tm* books list the attractions on each major road in the states of AZ, CO, NM, and UT. He has also created two books for teaching *Tour Guiding* to those that want to learn the trade, or get licensed as a *Professional Tour Guide*.

This guidebook is one of many tourist guidebooks that Bill has produced for visitors to the western and southwestern states. You can find each described on Amazon.com Kindle e-books

Search Kindle under William C. McElroy and William (Bill) C. McElroy. Below are some of the e-books you might find interesting and enjoy.

 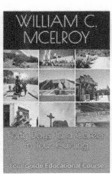  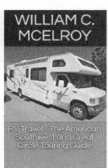

 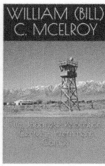 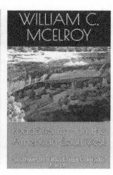 

Cover

Mt. Lemmon, Tucson, Arizona a popular spot for summer and winter fun, Oktoberfest, day camping and picnics, skiing, and hiking the mountain trails.

The Tucson summers are hot, usually over 100 degrees each day from June to September, but Mt. Lemmon is approximately 20 to 30 degrees cooler due to its elevation and tree abundant forest. In the winter, when Tucson is 70 to 80 degrees, Mt. Lemmon may be at 30 degrees with a layer of snow, thus one can go skiing there.

Made in the USA
Coppell, TX
01 December 2023